HEARTS AND MINES

HEARTS AND MINES

With the Marines in Al Anbar:
A Story of Psychological
Warfare in Iraq

RUSSELL SNYDER

CASEMATE
Philadelphia & Oxford

Published in the United States of America and Great Britain in 2012 by
CASEMATE PUBLISHERS
908 Darby Road, Havertown, PA 19083
and
10 Hythe Bridge Street, Oxford, OX1 2EW

Copyright 2012 © Russell Snyder

ISBN 978-1-61200-105-0
Digital Edition: ISBN 978-1-61200-117-3

Cataloging-in-publication data is available from the Library of Congress
and the British Library.

10 9 8 7 6 5 4 3 2 1

Printed and bound in the United States of America.

For a complete list of Casemate titles please contact:

CASEMATE PUBLISHERS (US)
Telephone (610) 853-9131, Fax (610) 853-9146
E-mail: casemate@casematepublishing.com

CASEMATE PUBLISHERS (UK)
Telephone (01865) 241249, Fax (01865) 794449
E-mail: casemate-uk@casematepublishing.co.uk

Except where noted, all photographs author's collection.

CONTENTS

For Nichole, in fulfillment of a promise.
For the men of the United States Marine Corps.
For the people of Al Qa'im.
For peace.

In fallow fields the wheat still grows
Though no one comes to tend the rows
But tanks and soldiers as they sweep
Across the barren plain and seek
To sow a seed of hope
For evil still pervades this land
Grasping with a withered hand
The breath of men from far away
Who wait upon their Judgment Day
In hopes that each by God is blessed
As they confront their greatest test
Of courage and morality
Where everyone has lost a friend
Each man looks forward to the end
Searching for a reason why
So many people here must die
Before shafts of wheat may rise once more
And beauty to the land restore

AL QA'IM, IRAQ
2005

Author's Note

The names of individuals throughout this book have been changed to protect their identities. Dialogue, where it appears, has been constructed from memory. Though quotations embody the spirit of what was said, they should not be considered exact transcriptions of conversations. I have attempted to recreate as faithfully as possible the actual events upon which this book is based from my own notes and memories, as well as the memories and resources of other participants, but it is possible others may present them differently. I am also deeply indebted to Richard Kane, my editor. His excellent work and professional wisdom have helped me to realize a better book. Any errors that remain are my own.

"Mankind must put an end to war, or war will put an end to mankind."
JOHN F. KENNEDY

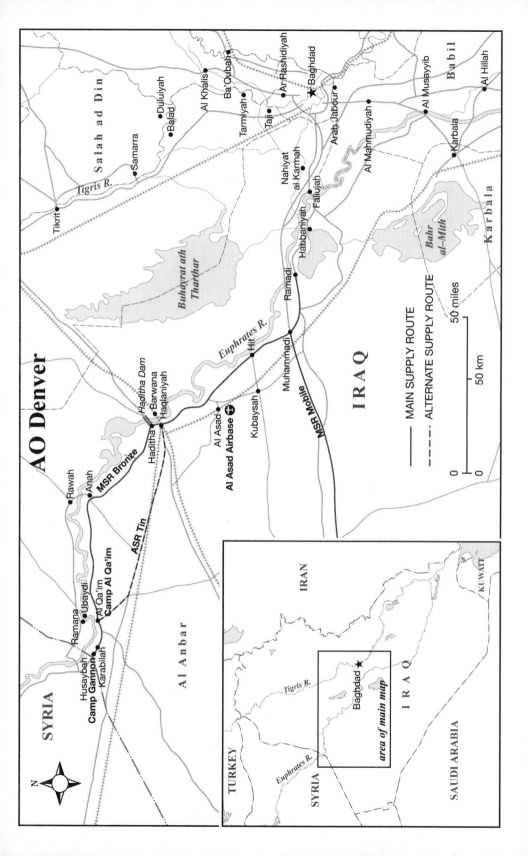

PREFACE

Four years have passed since I first was introduced to war. Four years have dulled my memories, and the emotions connected with them have faded. Yet the urge to purge my mind of those unforgettable days that have since and forever influenced my attitude on life, to come to terms with the weight upon my conscience, still gnaws at the edge of my waking mind. Several times I have started and failed to complete this written record of my experience, having always dreaded the confrontation with painful remembrances and doubting whether my small part in the greater story constituted a portion much worth telling. In the twilight of my third deployment to Iraq, the personally held importance of doing so has not seemed to lessen. I know mine is not an uncommon story. I know that if I have suffered, I have not done so to any greater degree than many millions who have shared in the conflict since the war began in 2003, and certainly not more so than have the veterans of previous wars. There are many dead men whose stories deserve to be told more than mine. The triviality, the selfishness, of sharing my small role feels almost shameful. But I can no longer deny my compulsion to complete this task, to glean from the pages of my wartime journal a work worthy of preserving the memory of the lives destroyed around me. I hope as well that the peace I seek may come if I can at last give voice to my thoughts and account to myself, to whatever constitutes my feeling of the presence of God, and to the ghosts of war.

This is the story of my preliminary wartime experience. These are my memories of life as a member of one of the U.S. Army's three-man tactical psychological operations teams (TPTs). While attached in support of the United States Marine Corps' 3rd Battalion, 2nd Marines, and 3rd Battalion, 25th Marines, operating along the Euphrates river valley in western Iraq's Anbar desert during the spring and summer of 2005, I witnessed what was at that time some of the most vicious counterinsurgency fighting of Operation Iraqi Freedom since Fallujah.

I do not claim to be a historian, or even to have been privy to the big picture of the war reserved for the generals and their staff. Nothing I did was heroic or changed the course of history or any battle. Mine was the perspective of a low-ranking sergeant, isolated from the media's reports and influenced by the stresses of fatigue, fear, and moral uncertainty. Doubtless there are details in the collective record of the war's participants I am unaware of or have forgotten. Others may remember the same events differently. Some things, as well, should frankly not be said. But as for the memories of one soldier who was there, what follows is what really happened.

INTRODUCTION

I have stopped dreaming so often of the war. I can't remember when exactly, but one night, to my relief, the nightmares didn't come again. It was the first night in months, ever since my return from Iraq to the United States, that I hadn't revisited the dusty streets of Anbar in my sleep. The faces of dead friends and strangers remain clear in my mind's eye as I write, but I am no longer haunted by them. They live on with the feeling of a smooth, warm stone in the pit of my stomach: not uncomfortable, but never quite forgotten. Neither are the events of my first eight months in Iraq, for I decided early in the deployment I would make a journal entry each day to preserve the experience for myself and perhaps to communicate my daily thoughts to my family in the event of my death.

It is not that I had any particular fear of dying, because I did not understand death. Rather, a strange fascination with mortality had begun to haunt my thoughts over the past months. Previously, I'd not known more than a handful of people who'd died, but as that reality changed, so too did my youthful perception of myself as invulnerable. My friend Jon had been a member of the company my unit replaced, and just a few months before our arrival lost his life when a suicide car bomber attacked his team in the same area my team would later be assigned to patrol. After arriving at the dead men's former base, I walked into their office in the abandoned train station at Al Qa'im and discovered a small but poignant collection of reminders that they had never returned.

Most of the three men's personal effects had of course been packed up and shipped to their next of kin, but left behind were a few items like the heavy black power converter upon which someone had written the numbers *Nine-Five-One* with a white paint marker.

Nine-Five-One signified belonging to the first team, of the fifth detachment, of the army's Ninth Psychological Operations Battalion. To the Marines or soldiers who packed up Jon's things and forgot the converter, they meant nothing more, but to me, the numbers meant my friend had touched the object, used it to charge his laptop or his music player, and never been back to take it home with him. They reminded me of his face, a memory that would never age. Years after his death I still remember Jon as I last saw him, alive and smiling in the glow of a backyard campfire, surrounded by the friends who loved him. I think of the young family he left behind, and the arguments we never resolved. The legacy of his life, a speck among the millions death has claimed through war, one I took for granted, deserved to be counted as more than just a number. It was a life worth remembering, and the loss of it forced me to confront the keen possibility that I, too, might die.

I kept my journal not because I expected to die, but because I'd learned to accept that death came unexpectedly. I wanted to leave a record of my existence, a proof of my worth as a human being should I never have a chance to leave behind anything better than a dog-eared composition notebook. Any small effort to encapsulate the last days of my life, however pathetic, would better help me fend off the shadow of death than I could by simply ignoring my fear. While the journal remained unfinished, I could not fall prey to a deadly sense of complacent fatalism.

Writing down what happened also helped me come to terms with ideas that at the time I could ill afford to dwell upon. It was a conscious attempt to wipe my mind clean and stay focused on my daily responsibilities. But even now, reminiscing from the safety of my own home, a sense of unease remains as I thumb the notebook's soiled pages. I've come to realize the memories will never fully die, and the changes in my psyche will likely never be undone.

From the perspective of its participants, war unfolds in such a brutally disturbing fashion that after one experiences it firsthand, it is hard to understand why so often war's slaughter is still romanticized in film and literature as an honorable expression of patriotism. There are long periods of boredom punctuated by incidents of such gut-wrenching savagery, such barbarism, that one wonders how it is that either side can ever call itself "peacekeepers" or to be carrying out the will of God.

Having seen war in its raw form, stripped of its romantic euphemisms, my perception has morphed from one of callously accepting it as a part of human nature to understanding it as an unconscionable, outdated, barbaric practice. It's a worrisome flaw humanity has yet to overcome that in our modern age we still accept the butchery of our human brothers and sisters as a means of settling our politicians' and religious leaders' disagreements.

Yet, there are also reminders that life persists in the midst of such madness. Farmers patiently attempt to coax the crops that feed their families from destroyed fields, choosing to stay while their neighbors flee, whether from a stubborn denial of how dangerous their neighborhoods have grown, a fear of losing their land, or the absence of the choice or means to leave as well. Soldiers browse the shelves of their camp stores with no intention of buying anything other than a few minutes of diversion, as the only goods for sale are the same untouched stacks of tampons and wrong size T-shirts that have gathered dust for weeks. Birds sing each morning to greet the new dawn, oblivious to, or perhaps in spite of, the destruction around them. It is a nasty business, and through millennia, regardless of how advanced the tools used to do the job become or how logical the rhetoric to sell it to the public, the end result always remains the same.

Death.

We have, as a species, gotten very efficient in the art of destruction over the centuries, and even learned there are indeed a few things created through war, such as war profits, deep resentments, widows, nightmares, debt, and cripples.

I can only hope naïvely that through sharing the experiences remembered in this book, my pebble cast into the sea, I might raise the tide for future peace.

1. INTO THE OVEN

The feeling of being conscious of the weight of my heart and lungs the morning of my departure for Iraq remains with me, more so than any image or smell. It is a mood I struggle to name, for it is not one that could have been called anticipation, anxiousness, excitement, or worry, although it included elements of each. My heart raced, and though I had no one to say goodbye to, I wished I did.

Strange, this wish to feel heartache.

I envied my friends for the arms around their necks and the tears shed for them by misty-eyed wives and girlfriends. Years later, having returned to Iraq for my second tour, I received a manila envelope myself as several of these men would; stamped with a lawyer's return address. But at the time I could not know what was to be, and so stood alone, unjaded, quietly empathizing.

It seemed as though the sun itself decided to take a longer route to work that day. Time moved in slow motion, but move it did, and the crisp, clear morning turned to day. This day, the culmination of months of late nights crawling through cold, red North Carolina mud, of firing countless rounds through machine guns and pistols and rifles, of threading through pitch-dark forest trails in the cramped confines of our Humvees until the green and depthless static of our night vision goggles screamed inside our brains, had come at last. No longer could we rely on the tacit reassurance that after our imagined deaths, we would be resurrected to participate in the next exercise. The long-awaited day's weighty presence hung about our shoulders like a lead blanket.

My thoughts echoed in my skull the same way our speaker truck broadcasts had reverberated through the pockmarked walls of the mockup villages we'd patrolled with the Marines in California's desert country, the same men with whom we were about to be reunited in Iraq.

Had we gotten enough of the shooting ranges, battle drills, and medical training to fully arm us with the skills we needed to survive?

No amount of training had saved the lives of the dead men from the company we were ordered to replace. Everything seemed to be over too quickly. The enemy, unlike the role-players we'd been fighting, would not shoot paint rounds in Iraq's desert, and I wasn't convinced we were absolutely prepared to face real insurgents.

How were we to tell friend from nonuniformed foe, anyways, in the streets and alleys, among the crowds?

Until recently, it had all seemed like a game. I had followed the television's news reports with a distant interest until the deaths of people I knew shattered my cold indifference, but even then the war still never felt genuinely personal. Now, suddenly, it dawned on me that my name might one day soon be one of those printed in some small corner of my hometown newspaper, among the dead. The truth of danger loomed, inevitable, and I had still so many questions.

As reality sank in, a fog of doubt and shock muted the sounds around me. I stood in a tan sea of camouflage uniforms before the loading docks of our offices, a speck in the massed formation of the company, following commands as a robot would. After the prerequisite cliché-filled speeches from our leaders about fulfilling our place in history and serving the nation, we dispersed in search of one last hug to tide us over through the months ahead. I loaded my swollen duffle bag under one of the two glistening charter buses that had pulled into the parking lot behind us and climbed into a rear seat.

I watched my buddies crane their necks around the tall seat backs as they peered from deeply tinted windows, trying to pick out which of the waving hands outside was meant for them. Soon distance made their families very small, and as we sped along the interstate, the rumble-voiced motor coach sang a lonely lullaby to the accompaniment of its humming tires. Despite my mind's chaotic jumping and the stress of the morning, my head fell to my chest and I was overcome by an exhausted sleep.

I woke reluctantly as the bus ran over a seam in the road. Ahead of me, arms popped out of seats whose occupants had also been roused, and their owners yawned and stretched and began to murmur quietly among themselves. We entered a city. I leaned my cheek against the coolness of the window, waiting for a road sign, but I didn't need one. The ivory needle of the Washington Monument grew taller on the horizon, and a little further, the dome of the U.S. Capitol building. As a history buff, I laughed inwardly at the irony that I found the landmarks more interesting as a sign of our proximity to the airport rather than as symbols of our national heritage, especially since I'd never before seen them. My neck ached and I wanted to get out and walk the stiffness out of my legs.

The stark white of the capitol's dome against a slate gray sky was not the only contrast that drew my attention through the panorama of my window view. In the foreground of those storied monuments, manifestations of American power and government, neglected neighborhoods languished row on row, different versions of the same scene flickering like an antique film through the fences that lined the way. Black shadows of men in tattered coats gathered in the entryways of neighborhood liquor stores, clutching brown paper bags like dark stubborn sentries at the gates of a blighted kingdom. Helping hands, if they looked for any, must have been far removed, and certainly did not come from a government that chose instead to spend its billions on an endless, meandering war declared only against the intangible concept of terror. There had been another similarly named war fought here, too, during the Johnson administration: one on poverty. But that one had never been as well funded as the current conflict, and judging by the scenery, had ended in defeat. For a long time, it seemed, the men had resigned themselves to being forgotten.

The sentries who greeted us at the airport were tightly permed, white-haired old ladies in blue vests. One kind grandmother handed me a sandwich baggie stocked with toothpaste and baby wipes, bidding me a teary good-bye as if I were her own son. I could not help feeling like an imposter. In her lifetime she may well have sent off her natural-born son to Korea or

Vietnam. Perhaps she had lost him and searched now for a glimpse of his face in our uniformed host to soften her pain. It was an oddly awkward sendoff, and I, for one, could shed no sympathetic tears for such well-meaning strangers. I felt only embarrassment, not as a hero deserving of the applause showered on us by these silver haired Samaritans and their parchment-skinned hands. Our uniforms drew stares and whispers from the civilian travelers around us. I blended as best I could into the anonymous parade of brown boots and backpacks as we negotiated the gauntlet of security and settled in for the long flights ahead.

From Baltimore we flew to ports first in England, Germany, and finally to an Air Force base in Qatar, waking only to change planes as there was little else to do but sit and wait. The relative comfort of traveling on commercial airliners as opposed to the military transports we might normally have expected had done little to prevent the stiff joints I rubbed on the way into a vast hangar cooled by extremely loud, giant industrial fans. Long wooden benches arranged in rows had long since been worn smooth by thousands of numb bottoms. I dozed with my head back on my Kevlar helmet pillow, halfway between consciousness and coma, occasionally scratching the backs of my fingernails over the shadow of an oily sandpaper beard that had since our departure begun to sprout relentlessly from my chin.

The instructions of some half-inaudible announcement blaring over the intercom startled me from my fitful nap. I strained to discern them, but no one else seemed to pay much attention. Through my boots I could feel the vibration of the concrete hangar floor as it shook under the prop blast of our long-anticipated transport to Iraq, a C-130 military cargo plane. I shuffled sleepily up the lowered tail ramp through a warm pungent breeze of kerosene fumes, wedged myself into place on a red nylon web seat, and grabbed the two ends of my seatbelt before the man in line behind me sat down and pinned me in. We shared tight quarters, shoulder to shoulder with our backs against the skin of the aircraft, even tighter now that we all wore helmets and body armor. A line of sand-colored shipping containers that stored the company's equipment walled off the central aisle. I stared intently into the depthless panel of the one in front of me until it hurt my eyes, and as the plane droned on, my head dropped again into unconsciousness.

The man beside me nudged me awake as he readjusted himself to don his helmet. Burning bulbs studded at intervals along its length bathed the bay in a blood-red glow. Loudspeakers crackled with the proclamation that we had entered Iraqi airspace. An air of whispery restlessness swirled throughout the cabin.

I clutched the edge of my seat as the aircraft began a steep descent. The pilot nosed down sharply, trying to limit our potential exposure to enemy surface-to-air fire. Outside, the normal low buzzing of the props rose to a high-pitched whine and the rising G forces pushed me low in my seat. Just when I began to feel sick, our angle of approach leveled off sharply and the plane's tires bumped tarmac with a screech. My neighbors' shoulders mashed into mine as the engines roared in full reverse. As we came to a stop, an audible collective sigh of relief accompanied the metallic screeching of brakes, with the realization we'd landed safely in Iraq at the Marine Corps' Al Asad Air Base without any extra holes in the airplane. Or maybe ours was a sigh of resignation. We'd crossed our Rubicon. There could be no turning back for many months.

No lights were visible outside as the black hole above the ramp opened on a starless void, but it was not an empty darkness. At the edge of the airfield I could just make out the shadowy silhouettes of several open-backed cargo Humvees, and as we filed closer under the burden of our rucksacks, their occupants dismounted to approach us. The drivers wore night vision goggles tilted up on their helmets. I hoped they could see better than I the winding curves and dark high walls of the canyon road we sped along on the way to an uncertain destination.

My eyes flashed open as though my dream had suddenly stopped playing on a television set gone unexpectedly dark during a thunderstorm. A puff of fine white dust hung in the air around the door jamb of our small white room, set adrift by the pressure wave of an explosion that still echoed in the distance.

I propped myself up on an elbow and turned to reassure myself the rest of my team was alright. Cat, the leader of our small team, sat already awake and dressed on his bed across the room, watching a movie on his laptop computer. He seemed unperturbed as he noticed my startled reaction and adjusted his baseball cap. He had been to Iraq before, during the invasion, so I grudgingly accepted his assurance the noise had been only outgoing artillery and nothing to worry about. Josh, our driver, woke at the same time. He pulled his scratchy military-issue blanket over his head and sank back on his bunk bed in the corner. He lay motionless for a minute, then groggily threw his legs over the edge of the mattress and climbed down to the floor and slid his feet into a pair of rubber sandals. He flipped a towel over his shoulder and shuffled to the door with slow inaccurate steps, lifting a hand to shield his eyes as he cracked the door. A thick wave of hot air rolled off the gravel pathway outside and washed over me, filling my nose with the scent of dry, ancient dust.

It had been hot in Qatar, too, in the days before we'd finally reached Iraq, and felt hotter because the desert sun's baking rays radiated back from every blindingly white surface. The omnipresent concrete bunkers, the crushed, monochromatic gravel paving the whole world to the horizon, even the sky itself seemed covered with a film of powdery sand that made the kilometer-long trek to the chow hall seem akin to walking through a painfully brilliant field of freshly fallen snow. Iraq seemed only slightly better.

The heat rushed over my face and brought back childhood memories of standing at my mother's side, eagerly looking into the oven as she checked her baking. Here though, the heat lasted forever and there were no cookies to look forward to afterward.

I lay on my side and rubbed morning grit from my eyes, taking in the unadorned white sheet-metal walls of my bedroom. During the night I had stumbled through darkness and collapsed on the first empty mattresses my outstretched hand could find. The bed was cheap-looking foam but not uncomfortable compared to the airport floors and bench seats of the previous few days. No other furniture decorated the room save for two bunk beds and another single bed, one in each corner. One of the top bunks still wore its factory wrapping of clear plastic. A fine layer of baby powder-like dust frosted every flat surface. Where we'd stepped, our boot prints stitched the floor like tracks of wild game across a muddy riverbank.

I yawned and glanced back over at Cat. He looked every bit the New Yorker he proudly proclaimed himself to be, stereotypically brash and Italian, with dark curly hair and frequently voiced opinions. To hear him tell it, one would think he hailed from the mean streets of Little Italy, but in actuality, he'd grown up in a small town upstate. Under his cap, his hair still glistened with dampness. I wondered what the showers were like.

Even through the rubber soles of my flip flops, the ground warmed my feet as I crunched through the gravel toward the shower trailer. On the way I passed Josh, towel in hand. He raised his eyebrows and gave me a look I couldn't quite interpret, as if I should prepare myself for something unpleasant. But the shower proved refreshing, if rather Spartan and public.

At least it existed; I could be thankful for that. Who knew what the facilities would be like outside the main base?

Morning rituals completed, the three of us stepped outside the room dressed in our desert camouflage, and Cat locked our door with the only key we'd been given. A couple of guys from the detachment already waited, sitting on the wooden pallets that served as porches in front of our line of trailers, smoking cigarettes. The warm air hovered around us, unusually stagnant. Exhaled smoke hung in a wispy veil in the alley way. Further down, someone had strung a laundry line across the walkway that sagged under the weight of dusty wet clothes, sure to be dry soon. I recalled an illustration from a *National Geographic* story about shanty towns.

I heard footsteps at the mouth of the alley behind me and turned to see Gerry, our detachment chief, approaching with a set of keys in his hand. He had deployed early to Iraq as part of the advance party to arrange for the arrival of the rest of the detachment, so it was the first time we had seen him in nearly two weeks. Those of us who were newly arrived stood to meet him and exchanged greetings and handshakes in turn. He looked tired and serious, perhaps a bit grayer than before, but a spark in his eye betrayed his good mood and delight in seeing us together again. As usual, though, we were expected elsewhere, and Gerry cut the conversation short to lead us to a nearby lot bordered by a low wall of earth-filled wire and felt boxes called HESCO barriers, named for the Hercules Engineering Solutions Consortium, which produced them.. Weaving a path between armored Humvees and a hodgepodge of decrepit-looking civilian vehicles, we stopped beside a dust-covered passenger van and waited for Gerry to unlock the doors. It was stifling inside. The boss flipped a switch and a feeble flow of lukewarm air puffed from the vents.

I leaned against my window in the middle seat, feeling the hot breeze on my skin and trying to memorize the route. The same shade of dull grayish tan painted land, road, lampposts, and bushes the color of the plume of dust kicked up by the van, except where other vehicles' tires had scrubbed the dust from the road. The two black ribbons of asphalt stretched past a repetitive panorama of the skeletons of dead trees and unremarkable flat roofed buildings. We passed a row of shrapnel-pocked airplane hangars nestled inside man-made valleys along a broad runway, witness to the attacks early in the war that had crippled Saddam's air forces. Scattered at intervals in the distance, the broken noses of MiG fighters from those hangars poked out from berms of sand bulldozed around them in a vain attempt to hide them from American bombs.

The van slowed to take a sharp corner around a pair of portable toilets and rolled to a stop in a parking lot hidden within the courtyard of a cluster of the same type of flat-roofed concrete buildings. Carefully stacked sandbags blocked their deep-silled windows. Arabic slogans and colorful murals of Iraqi pilots and jets in flight decorated the stucco walls on both sides of the entry way. Gerry noted casually that the building had once been a training facility for officers of the Iraqi Air Force, recently reconfigured to serve as Tactical PSYOP Detachment 950's headquarters in the Anbar province. Two T-shirt-clad soldiers stood on the roof, waving for us to enter. One of them had been a roommate of mine during language school. I flashed a smile and waved back.

The ceiling impressed me most. It was dim inside, and my eyes took a few seconds to readjust from the bright sunlight. Once they did, I admired the intricate geometric patterns cut into the plaster of the ceiling and hidden behind crudely built plywood shelves stocked with boxes of Kool-Aid powder and paperback novels. Mosaic tiled floors still shone with tarnished elegance beneath my boots. An unlit and slightly damaged crystal chandelier rather ironically decorated the next room.

From the doorway, an unfamiliar black captain with a glistening bald head motioned for us to follow him to a corner dominated by a large map of western Iraq. Judging by his mannerisms I could sense his eagerness to deliver his presentation. I suppose it was just that he looked forward to finally going home. The briefing marked a milestone that signaled the end of his deployment, and the beginning of mine. The same restless energy emanated from a group of fifteen or so soldiers already gathered around the map, some of them members of my detachment, others veterans of the outgoing detachment curious to see the faces of the men who would take their place.

In spite of the unspoken significance it held for both groups, the meeting was unduly long and uninteresting. Nothing we hadn't heard a hundred times before in the situation reports and cultural studies we had pored over in the months prior to arrival. The captain with the shiny head asked if we had any questions. There were none.

My leg had fallen asleep from leaning back on a countertop. I followed the rest of the group back outside into the sun-baked parking lot, clumping along woodenly as the sensation returned to my limb. One of the other detachment's soldiers waited behind a disassembled M2 machine gun he had just removed from the turret of a nearby Humvee.

The M2 had been used in World War II as aircraft armament. I hefted the yard-long detached barrel in my hands, surprised by its heft. It was the first time since basic training I had even seen a "Ma Deuce," as we sometimes called the gun. At our base in North Carolina, we never trained on the heavy guns because there were none in the unit's inventory. Similarly, the soft-skinned Humvees we were accustomed to driving were nothing like the beast parked on the curb before us, squat under the weight of its own armor.

Ordinarily the only armament atop our loudspeaker trucks at that time was the M249 Squad Automatic Weapon (SAW), a normally hand-carried, belt-fed machine gun firing a .223 (5.56mm) cartridge, a caliber commonly used by squirrel hunters and the standard for NATO infantry. It was intentionally small, designed to maim rather than kill and had come into the American inventory with the adoption of the M16 rifle during the Vietnam War. Many of the men in our company vocally resented the fact we weren't equipped with more powerful weapons to defend our vehicles. I hoped when we got to wherever we were going, we could convince the armorer to lend us a heavier weapon, but in the interim I would have to content myself with learning how to care for this one first.

The instructor called our attention to a white bed sheet laid on the ground in front of him, on which he had arranged the black shining entrails of the gun in neat rows. It was hard to imagine how everything went back together, there were so many pieces. They did though, simply enough, and in an hour or two we had all mastered disassembling and reassembling the heavy weapon, loading, cleaning, and the technique of using a small flat tool to verify the proper space between the barrel and receiver.

When class ended, we retired to the shade of the headquarters building and thirstily gulped down bottles of cool water and powdered flavor drinks. I wandered the premises alone, investigating the building's dark corners and jumbled piles of boxes. From the open back doorway I heard cheers and sounds of a scuffle. Back home, the detachment had instituted a traditional friendly brawl we called "Match of the Day" to pass time when we were bored. The latest was apparently underway. I walked outside sipping my water and joined the ring forming around the two combatants. They were both soaked with sweat, their uniforms wrinkled and sand-spattered. We observers shouted over each other with suggestions how each fighter could better subdue his opponent. After an intense but indecisive struggle, one of their noses dripped blood and Gerry stopped the match to prevent the friendly contest from turning serious.

During my tour of the building, before being distracted by the brawl outside, I had seen stairs I wanted to follow. With the fighters weary and resting, a few other soldiers and I climbed to the roof to take in the surrounding view. On the road below, a shapely blonde Marine in short shorts ran past with her working dog, a German shepherd. From what I could see of the trash fires and rubble in the other three directions, she was the best scenery we would glimpse in a long time.

I woke up sweating. I lay motionless in bed, reluctant to move, beads of sweat trickling down my ribcage the way rain runs off a windshield. It had been weeks since I had been able to sleep in so late, and with the uncomfortable outdoor heat blistering through the thin metal wall of my bedroom, I wondered how I'd managed to, smothered as I was in my soaked bed sheets. The electricity must have gone out some time ago, and the air conditioner stood silent. Our room seemed eerily quiet without the usual constant humming, save for Josh's slow, measured breaths.

I stepped outside, being careful not to make too much noise. A cooling breeze provided some relief. It was actually hotter inside than out. I sat down on the edge of the wooden pallet and lay back with my eyes closed as the dry breeze blew up my shorts. The sun-soaked boards felt good through my T-shirt, but I could not relax. It was quiet enough to think, and I felt very far from home.

At the end of the alleyway, air conditioning units starting coming back on one by one and the surge of power rapidly reached the unit above my head. The fan clattered back to life. My moment of Zen gone, I exhaled deeply and went back inside to get my soap and towel.

While waiting for everyone else to get ready, I opened the lid of the black plastic footlocker I used to store my gear. My earlier moment of homesickness had made me thirsty for sun tea, the way my mother fixed it during my childhood. In the summers of my youth, she put a handful of tea bags in a glass jar painted with yellow flowers, and left it on the front porch to brew in the sun. I impatiently watched the water darken, but she always told me to wait. But how worthwhile the wait, on those warm Montana summer days, when at last I had an ice-filled glass, sweet and bitter at the same time. I'd learned to love her tea. When I made it myself, it reminded me of the carefree happiness I once knew.

I found the box of Lipton's under a folded stack of uniforms and pulled out two pouches. I folded the bags in half and stuffed them inside a plastic water bottle, leaving the strings out and screwing the top back on to hold them in place. I smiled to myself, tasting the memory of tea and wondering what sort of comments the guys would make when they walked back from the shower and saw my murky bottle sitting in the gravel outside my doorway.

The detachment's eleven o'clock appointment was with a Marine Corps master gunner, an expert in weapons and the fundamentals of rifle marksmanship. As with every unit arriving in the Iraqi theater, ours fulfilled a number of mandatory training requirements during the reception and integration period. The long list included a review of the rules of engagement, the laws of war, prohibited targets, Iraqi customs, and weapons drills. Gerry led us on a short hike past the chow hall and a line of ubiquitous low tan buildings, stopping at one with a camouflage net draped over the doorway. He directed us to a classroom lined with benches made from two-by-fours and left to find our instructor.

Master Guns finally arrived and sniffed into the room swaddled in the airy, condescending aloofness of a man proud of his rank. We reciprocated by politely pretending we weren't bored out of our minds reviewing the same material for the thirtieth time.

Maybe the army and Marine Corps were not so different after all.

When he finished, our instructor gave us a time to come back the next day, so we might put what we had learned into practice at the rifle range.

It was dusk, and buggy. Sand flies, clouds of them, preferred the evening's cooler temperatures. With every step back to my trailer, the tiny pests darted around my face and bit my neck. I slapped reflexively to kill them and walked with Josh down the alley to the interpreters' trailer, next to our own.

I had been trained in Korean as part of my coursework after graduating the Psychological Operations course and had gotten more proficient during several deployments to Korea. Unfortunately my language skills were nowhere near to qualifying me as a translator, and even if I had been any good, knowing the language didn't help me in Iraq.

After years of war, most of the battalion's few Arabic-trained speakers had already been on multiple deployments. In an attempt to make the deployment cycle more equitable for all soldiers, the Fourth PSYOP Group began to transfer members from battalions that usually dealt with Europe, South America, and Asia into the solitary tactical battalion. Charlie Company, my company, was mostly composed of soldiers freshly drafted from these other battalions. Even those few soldiers in the company who had been through the Arabic course were not very adept in communicating with native Arabic speakers, so we were forced to rely on translators.

Without them, the ability to accomplish our assigned mission would have been very limited. Our task as Psychological Operations specialists was to influence the behavior and emotions of the Iraqi public into accepting America's occupation of their country, and in every conceivable forum, covert and overt, whether in leaflets, conversation, radio, newspapers, or the internet, we needed to be able to convey our messages in the language of our target audience. The cultural expertise and cooperation of our native translators lent more legitimacy to our presence and our propaganda than anything else we could have ever claimed to do.

The door to the interpreters' room hung open, wagging slightly on silent hinges. A tall olive-skinned man with dark, deep-set eyes stood in the doorway smoking a cigarette. He cracked a wry smile, inviting Josh and me into the circle of men huddled cross-legged around a game of gin rummy on the floor. The space was colorfully decorated with landscape posters and a large oriental rug. In the corner, a small electric teapot whistled merrily. The man with the hollow eyes offered us a glass of tea.

The swirling flakes of my strong, dark drink settled to the bottom of my tiny glass. My new friend poured a generous helping of sugar from an unmarked paper bag into his own cup and offered me the rest.

We shared introductions, played cards, and joked. The men had been soldiers in Saddam's army, and students, and fathers. They were reserved in sharing their opinions of the political problems their country faced, but it couldn't be denied they were hospitable.

The rest were not so sinister looking as the man with the sunken eyes. I can only imagine the scenes that passed before those eyes to make them so joyless, but even in the relaxed setting he seemed restless and brooding, mostly watching the others. I usually prided myself on being open to unfamiliar cultures, but couldn't help secretly wondering about the loyalty and motives of these men, whose paths had led them to collaboration with an army that had so recently overthrown their own government.

One troll-like, hunchbacked man called himself "John," adding with a chuckle that in Arabic, "John" sounded like the word for ghost. He maintained a yellow-toothed smile while relating the story of how his entire family had been murdered by Saddam's regime. With an evil cackle he told me he hoped for revenge, and would kill any Sunnis he met if he had the chance. Later I learned John wore a ski mask when he worked, but I wonder if it was less to disguise his haggard face from those who would harm him than to hide his sectarian contempt.

One man did seem genuinely happy, a university student whose studies had been interrupted by the war. "Rick" sported a goatee, uncommon among his peers. Most other Iraqi men wore moustaches. He kept a bandanna wrapped around a thick head of curly black hair. His eyes shone behind his glasses with a flash of worldliness and intelligence, even optimism.

When we tired of cards, one of the men turned on the television and we watched the beginning of a poorly bootlegged movie with Arabic captions. Occasionally a silhouette of one of the theater patrons walked across the bottom of a tilted screen. The muddled sound made the story hard to follow. But in spite of the movie's laughably poor quality, the television flickered with the glow of normalcy. I hadn't watched one in ages, and everywhere I turned stared back another strange reminder of the distance from home. Even so, it wasn't long before the novelty wore off and my mind began to wander, worrying more about the unforeseen challenges of the deployment ahead and the home in the States I might never see again than with following the plot of the movie. I excused myself politely and left for bed.

Morning broke as it usually did, quickly. I rose early and walked to the shower trailer by the light of a predawn glow, but by the time I finished, the air already stirred with heat. Doors along the alley way opened and slammed shut as the other soldiers of the detachment readied themselves for the day ahead. Master Guns would be waiting for us at the rifle range, and he was not a man who would be pleased about being kept waiting. After a hurried breakfast we squeezed into our vans with arms full of armor and rifles and drove toward the base of a tall cliff at the perimeter of the camp, passing an abandoned blue-domed mosque and shady rows of olive trees.

An empty range greeted our arrival. No Master Guns, no vehicles, just a broad expanse of flat, bare ground and a long line of square wooden target frames waiting silently at the base of a sand berm. We parked the vans and clambered into the sunlight, wondering if perhaps we were not in the right place. The scant shade of a stand of date palms beckoned. We milled about there unconcerned, while the smokers puffed their cigarettes, but did not have to wait long. A convoy of armored Humvees approached from the opposite direction and backed into position to form a neat line on one side of the parking area. Master Guns emerged from the lead vehicle and gathered his Marines in a horseshoe formation around him while another group hurried to set up paper silhouettes in the target frames.

After briefing safety procedures and explaining how the range would operate, he directed everyone to the back of one of the Humvees that guarded the ammunition so we could load our magazines.

Master Guns demonstrated how we should approach the targets. He advanced toward the line in a smooth crouch, rifle leveled. With his arms hooked under his rifle, his intent stare, and the crouching gait, he reminded me of a Tyrannosaurus rex stalking its prey. After several dry runs proved our understanding of the technique, we graduated to using live ammunition.

Master Guns referred to the exercise as a failure drill, so called because it ensured the failure of the heart, lung, and brain functions of the individuals we mimed shooting. On command I walked forward, firing two shots into the chest and one in the head of the target in rapid succession each time Master Guns blew his whistle. The most cynical members of our detachment referred to the technique as putting "two in the heart, one in the mind," a callous affirmation of the challenges that faced a force charged with winning over the hearts and minds of a nation resentful of its occupation by foreign troops. Again and again we repeated the same movements, building muscle memory and reinforcing our performance of the drill as an automatic response.

On breaks I drank entire liter bottles of body-temperature water. Stinging sweat ran into my eyes from under my helmet. By the time we were released from the range around four in the afternoon I felt numb, as if all the electrolytes had drained from my body. My muscles were sore from the weight of my armor and the last remnants of my energy rapidly evaporated in the oppressive heat.

I splashed a handful of water onto my face and neck.

I hope I get used to this heat.

I would have taken off my armor before getting back in the van, but it was easier to wear it on the walk back to the room than carry it. As soon as I crossed the threshold I released the Velcro closure on my chest and let the vest slide onto the floor with a thud. My uniform top could not have been more soaked if someone poured a bucket of salty water over me. I peeled it off and lay back on my bed bare-chested, boots and all, closed my eyes and reveled in the beautiful coolness of the air conditioning.

Two hours later Gerry opened the door and stepped inside to inform us he had gotten word our team had been assigned to support the 3rd Battalion, 25th Marines, a unit of reservists from Ohio, and we should be leaving for their base at the Haditha Dam sometime the next day. Cat would need to find space on a convoy. Josh and I looked at each other, wordless, but with mutual understanding. We both knew that tomorrow, everything would be different. For us, the war was just beginning.

2. A SOFT BREATH OF TERROR

America owns the night.

So goes the army's claim, and on its battlefields our military relies on night vision goggles and thermal scopes for a distinct technological edge during nighttime operations against less well-equipped insurgents. The supply convoys from Al Asad to Haditha typically departed after nightfall to take advantage of the cover of darkness, and so Josh, Cat, and I had the day to ourselves while waiting for dusk. Big as it was, the camp did not offer much in the way of entertainment, but we were too anxious to be able to tolerate wasting the day sitting in our room. Hours ticked relentlessly by as we rifled through stacks of pirated DVDs at the shops outside the small post exchange and rode the Korean-built shuttle buses aimlessly in hopes of discovering someplace new. Finally we were obliged to grudgingly walk back to our trailer to pack our things. One of the other team leaders gave us a ride in the van to meet our convoy at the gate as the last light of day cast long shadows.

I had been expecting to ride in a vehicle more enclosed for my first trip outside the wire, and was surprised when the convoy leader directed us to the back of a cargo Humvee with a box of quarter-inch steel plate welded around three sides of the truck bed. At least I would not be alone with my uneasiness, exposed to the open air. Six Marines already seated on benches in the back seemed to quietly endorse the safety of the vehicle, as none of them showed any concern, although they, as I, may have been too proud to do so. One of them extended his hand to help Cat and me climb in with our rucksacks. Josh and Ali, our freshly assigned interpreter, rode in one of the trucks further forward.

Once situated, I unzipped the green nylon bag that protected my night vision goggles and fixed the support arm to my helmet mount. Looking outward proved an awkward operation, as I had to turn around and kneel on the bench with one foot in the bed of the truck. There were cutouts for rifle barrels in the steel walls, but the only Marine who seemed concerned with security manned the SAW mounted just behind the Humvee's cab, aimed to the left of our direction of travel. If anything serious happened, we would be alerted by his firing soon enough. All the same, I had a strong, creeping sense of paranoia as the truck lurched forward and followed the convoy out the gate. I couldn't help constantly turning around to look outward.

Enough light reflected off the sky to make out the darkening shapes of Saddam's destroyed MiG fighters scattered in the desert on each side of the highway, dozens of them, out of place, with broken wings dipped in the sand. After a few miles they stopped appearing and the desert seemed at once more featureless and foreboding. Every pile of dirt seemed to be a potential hiding place for the roadside bombs that had recently featured so prominently in the news and intelligence reports. When we left the gate, Cat and I had been chatting with the Marines, but now we drove on in silence.

The drivers did not burn their headlights. I held my hand in front of my face, wondering if I really saw it or if the shadow was just my imagination. By now even the moon hid itself, and the only light visible came from stars and the faint red string of blackout taillights on the vehicles ahead of us in the convoy. They looked eerily like a procession of wide-set demon eyes. I flipped down my night vision goggles. Their weight dragged my helmet down low over my eyes, and I fumbled tightening the straps until it sat stable and comfortably.

The demon eyes were almost blinding through the intense magnification of my night vision goggles. Looking up, I marveled as I always did at how many usually unseen stars bejeweled the heavens. On the other side of the cargo bed, the shining eyes of those Marines who weren't wearing goggles blinked blindly with widely dilated pupils. Everything was quite distinct. I could clearly see the line of our vehicles barreling through a haze of dust, and on the crest of a hill, a cluster of buildings straddling the road. My throat tightened.

Lights burned in the windows of the village, and as we entered, the townspeople stepped aside warily. A group of men in long *dishdasha* robes stood gathered around a corner storefront, eyeing us, their drawn features highlighted under the harsh fluorescent glow. None of them smiled. They gave the kind of looks that made one feel unwelcome. We sized each other up quietly, the solemn men engaged in their evening social ritual and the nervous young warriors dressed like outlandish spacemen with the black machinery of our goggles protruding from our faces. My head spun on a swivel. Each approaching alleyway or piece of trash on the roadside made my heart beat faster, but the convoy continued into the night unmolested through the outskirts of the village. I allowed myself to relax, just a little, and breathe a sigh of relief.

Suddenly a staccato burst of machine gun fire rang out. My head dropped lower behind the steel plate, panning back and forth, watching for a muzzle flash. The back of the truck bristled with rifle barrels hastily turned outward. I could hear the radio in the cab crackling with transmissions and the metal-on-metal scratching of the Marines' rifles scanning for targets. Our SAW gunner keyed the Motorola on his shoulder to ask for a report, but no new fires broke the stillness of the night. The convoy sped on.

The lead vehicle had spotted a quad bike pacing the convoy on a parallel road across the canal and fired a burst to discourage its following us. Our SAW gunner relayed that the man driving it had not been killed, but dumped the quad on its side and wasn't following us anymore.

"Most likely," he laughed, "the man went home to change his shorts."

Some time later, having not seen any more vehicles, I noticed a portion of the sky near the horizon had no stars in it. The nearer we got the larger the section of starless sky became. It occurred to me we were close to arriving at the base of the dam, which at around eight stories tall blotted out the sky as a huge, looming shadow. My only frame of reference as far as dams were concerned had been small ones spanning the Missouri River back home in Montana. I had not expected to encounter such a huge structure in the middle of the desert! The roar of rushing water grew louder as the convoy slowly rolled to a halt at the very base of the megalith.

The Marines unhinged the truck's back gate and quickly dismounted. The SAW gunner took down his weapon and in a matter of seconds disappeared too, leaving Cat and me standing alone behind an empty truck. All around us the night hummed with running Marines and shouted orders, and above everything, the roar of the dam.

The dam swarmed very much like an anthill. After linking up with Josh and Ali we easily followed a line of Marines through the dark to a central stairway. Cat asked one of them where to find the first sergeant's office.

Getting upstairs was like driving in rush-hour traffic: slow going. On both sides of the stairwell, Marines muscled boxes of equipment and weapons between floors. The narrow stairwells and landings crowded with men forced to wait for a path to open up behind the boxes. Those of us waiting below warily watched the movers struggle with their awkward loads up the steep passageway, mindful of the fact that we had nowhere to move should one of them happen to fall.

Luckily, strong backs won out over gravity and the way cleared quickly. We located the command office, and Josh and I waited in the hallway with our bags while Cat went inside. A few moments later Cat followed the first sergeant back out. First Sergeant shook each of our hands and stated he was glad to have us as his guests, but Ali would have to stay with the Marines' other interpreters in a separate area as a security precaution.

Even when they wear our uniforms, no one trusts these men. I wonder if he feels like a prisoner.

The rest of us would lodge in a room at the end of the hall, which the first sergeant indicated with an outstretched finger. He called one of his Marines over to escort Ali to his quarters, and Josh followed to check that he got settled.

Our roommates didn't seem to be expecting us. They were still putting away their own things and stood about in various states of dress. Only one bed looked unoccupied among the two rows of bunks, and judging by their tired expressions, the current occupants weren't keen to add three more bodies to an already crowded space. After we explained the first sergeant had sent us, one of them yelled down the hall for one of his Marines to bring in another bunk bed. I left my bag on the floor and went to help, not wanting to seem lazy or take our hosts' hospitality for granted. My roommates were all staff sergeants, and I had seen them eyeing my three stripes with veiled condescension as if to question my right to sleep next to them. In their mind, I was still an unproven greenhorn with two strikes against me: I wasn't a Marine, and I wasn't *staff*.

On his way back to the room, Josh took over for the Marine who had been carrying the other side of the bunk bed with me. We set it up as quietly as we could, nearly impossible given the bed's metal legs and the concrete floor. Even though we made some horrible scrapes, the staff sergeants seemed to be either already asleep or ignoring us. I eased onto my creaky mattress, hopeful that tomorrow would lend the opportunity for some friendlier introductions and prove I wouldn't have to spend the rest of the deployment tiptoeing through a briar patch of Marine Corps rank and perceived disdain.

I smelled cigar smoke. One of the blacked-out screen doors at the other end of the room tapped its frame loosely in the breeze, and I could hear Cat and one of the staff sergeants talking on the balcony. They both looked up at something, puffing on their cigars. As I joined them, Cat gestured to the space above his head.

"Bats," he noted.

Dried guano of a colony of the sleeping creatures littered the floor of the balcony. Their tiny brown bodies twitched in a tightly huddled mass in the dark recesses of the underside of the balcony above. They didn't seem to be the blood-sucking type, but I gave them a wide berth and leaned over the edge of the retaining wall to see what lay below. A trio of soldiers in strange green uniforms walked abreast, toting Kalashnikovs, looking very small.

I had noticed a blue-, red-, and green-striped flag I didn't recognize flying next to the Iraqi and American flags atop the dam. These soldiers must be representatives of that nation sent to Iraq as part of the *Coalition of the Willing*. The smoking Marine, who called himself Tony, pointed out that Azerbaijani forces guarded the other side of the dam. The view to their post framed an unexpectedly beautiful desert panorama, an oasis of greenery and flying birds whose calls sweetened the morning air in concert with the rush of water from the floodgates below. A bloom of verdant grasses

and palm trees bordered the water's edge, softening the rift between the
river and a desert of sun-baked sand. Further down the spillway, a bridge
spanned the boundary where the river turned from frothy foam to cool,
clear water.

I was interested to observe that from my balcony, in the daylight, the
dam looked more like a huge hotel. American and Azerbaijani sides mir-
rored each other, with higher floors getting smaller and smaller until they
tapered to a point at the peak of the dam's retaining wall to form a right
triangle. On the way back from shaving, I'd seen diagrams of the place in
some of the books that littered the hallway, written both in Arabic and
what looked like Russian. Tony explained that army Rangers had thrown
anything of potential intelligence value into the hallways when they had
gone through, room by room, to seize the dam from the army of the former
regime. Ostensibly, intelligence specialists had long since combed through
them to pluck out anything of value, but years later the stacks still remained, piles upon piles of manuals written by the Yugoslav engineers who
had helped build the structure for Saddam, and reports full of numbers
left by the men who had operated it.

Gradually the activity at the base of the dam, where the trucks were
parked, began to increase. Marines turned their trucks to face back out
toward the road and made preparations for another mission, loading boxes
of MREs (meals ready to eat, those bland prepackaged meals that guarantee
constipation), water, and ammunition. This time, the convoy would include not only the new arrivals from Al Asad, but troops from the dam as
well. We new soldiers had missed out on a mission briefing held the day
before, but Tony assured us everything would go smoothly in spite of it
since our destination was only a short distance away.

Josh anticipated our imminent departure with the increasing commotion both outside and in, and returned with Ali to join our trio on the
balcony. Ali smiled as he recounted for us his memories of swimming and
fishing in the river below. The four of us followed Tony downstairs to find
a seat on the convoy to Barwanah.

The trip was short but nonetheless hot and monotonous. On the road
out from the dam, I watched a greasy, lazy plume of black smoke rising
from a trash fire, the only feature that stood out on an endless lunar plain
of broken rock blanketed by a cloudless sky.

Barwanah's outskirts were the same dull color as the ground the town sprouted from, as many of the buildings were actually constructed of dried mud brick. The convoy made a wide circle and came to a halt around a row of unfinished buildings. Piles of sand and brick haphazardly stacked sat within the rough outline of foundations.

Unfinished it may have been, but the town was not deserted. I saw several brown-skinned children darting around corners in the distance and peering curiously at our trucks. We were not the first visitors they had observed that day, it appeared. Already several armored vehicles blocked the roads into the village. In the shade of one of the buildings' courtyards I spotted the unmistakable silhouette of a Humvee-mounted loudspeaker. There were familiar faces there!

Josh, Cat, and I walked briskly toward the speaker truck that, in a few days, would be ours. I imagined the Bravo Company soldiers we were replacing would be glad to be rid of it.

The Marines had all recently exchanged their old-style uniforms for ones in a digital camouflage, so when they saw the old fashioned tan pattern of our uniforms, the PSYOP soldiers standing in the shade must have known we'd come for them. I expected to see more light in their faces, but though they shook our hands politely, the men looked worn down and tired.

Manny, the outgoing team leader, was a tall, stern-faced black man with a respectable sized bushy moustache. Over the next four days he would pass on a year's worth of insights and local contacts, he explained, starting with the mission to Barwanah.

While Cat and Manny continued to talk, Josh and I walked back to the speaker truck to speak with the gunner and driver. The gunner, Parm, had a moustache too, which made him look older than he probably was. Ordinarily not many soldiers in the States wear them, but here, the gunner explained from his turret, moustaches helped build rapport with the locals as a small symbol proving one's willingness to identify with their customs.

The locals were getting bolder now that they saw we were not kicking in doors or pulling anyone from their houses. At the edge of one of the buildings I saw a group of youngsters push a shy little boy into the open. At first he dragged his feet but was persuaded after much shoving by his friends to play on the bricks stacked in the courtyard, casting furtive glances at us and back to his comrades in the shade. Two more children ran out to join him. Parm handed Josh a bag of candy.

"Mistah, mistah!" cried the hawk-eyed kids, who forgot their shyness and ran toward us with grubby, outstretched hands and broad smiles. It was heartening to see the children's universal appreciation for sweets transcended any cultural differences between us.

Then, as easily as they swarmed out of the shadows, the children darted back into them. I turned to see a pair of Abrams tanks cresting the hill along the same street our convoy traced before to enter the town. The crew had painted the words "New Testament" on the main gun of the lead tank. Their treads ground through the dust with a metallic clanking and came to a stop behind a low wall, which hid the tanks but gave the turret gunners a clear view of the surrounding countryside as their massive main guns panned back and forth. They powered down their turbines and waited like lions for gazelles, unmoving, with only an occasional whirr or click to betray their presence.

Shortly after the tanks arrived, a black Opel sedan driven by a Marine led an open-backed Humvee into the shade where we stood. The Marines had been manning vehicle checkpoints before the convoy from Haditha arrived, and now returned to the fold with their bounty. The Humvee carried prisoners. Four blindfolded men stumbled from the vehicle and the Marines seated them on the ground with their backs to each other.

One of their guards called for Ali.

"Hey, Terp!"

With Ali's assistance, Cat and I questioned each of the men under the suspicious eyes of their captors.

What were they doing with so much money?

They had nearly five thousand dollars in American bills among them.

Where were they going?

The men asserted that they had been on their way to purchase a vehicle, and didn't understand why they'd been stopped. Most of them barely suppressed their visible anger, which only served to strengthen the Marines' doubts. They were left to sweat in the sun and questioned again thirty minutes later, this time by a specially trained interrogator who brought another translator with him. Their stories did not change, but in a wartime environment where such stories seemed suspicious, their alibi did not satisfy the Marines. The prisoners were stuffed back in the truck to await transportation to a detention facility.

After the prisoners had gone, the order came for everyone else to mount up and push further into Barwanah. Our element conducted a brief search of the town and seized a small arsenal of unauthorized weapons hidden in caches, including several cheaply made Balkan AK-47s and a World War II-era German Luger pistol stamped with the year 1938. The weapons proved the town was an area in which the enemy had been recently active, but when questioned, the townspeople refused to admit they had seen any insurgents.

"No Ali Baba," they replied, meaning no insurgents. "There are no problems here."

On one of the blue sheet-metal gates lining the main street, someone had drawn a picture in chalk of a twin-rotor Chinook helicopter being shot down by a kneeling man wielding a rocket launcher. I remembered reading about the actual crash, and the stickman seemed to be both a boast and a warning that we were unwelcome. The townspeople were either unwilling or too scared to help us or say anything that might later be interpreted as providing aid to the Americans.

The Euphrates River marked Barwanah's edge. Where the main street met the river, a rickety string of red pontoon boats bridged the distance across the water to her sister city of Haqlaniyah. There had once been a stone bridge, long ago, but all that remained were broken foundations. Our heavy trucks would be unable to safely cross the pontoon bridge, so the Marines commandeered a dilapidated white sedan and parked it lengthwise to block the opposite end. Before night fell it would be important to secure this approach. Haqlaniyah sat within shooting distance and we had no way of telling who waited for us there.

Josh, Cat, and I took up position on the roof of a building directly overlooking the bridge. Some Marines climbed the stairs with us and set up a machine gun and radio position on the retaining wall. Once we had established a watch roster, I returned downstairs to explore.

The owner of the house had been either a shopkeeper or a smuggler, evidenced by a small mountain of soft drinks and candy stashed in his front yard. Empty cans littered the ground around the pallets as his most recent guests helped themselves to his supply. Ali pawed through the refrigerator in the kitchen.

"Try some," he said.

He handed me a chunk of pita bread liberally spread with feta cheese. I noticed he left an American dollar on the shelf in place of the food he took. It was fresh and delicious, a welcome change of taste and texture from the MREs we had been eating. I munched as I walked around the kitchen, trying to savor it and hoping I wouldn't be sick later.

The kitchen door opened onto a portal to Eden. A flock of chickens clucked and pecked the grass busily beneath a canopy of grape vines trained into a living roof, the pillars of which were orange and peach trees. If I hadn't known better, I would have guessed I had stepped into a barnyard somewhere in the Mediterranean. A healthy-looking mother cow and her calf mooed softly in a corner. It seemed sad that such an idyllic and pastoral scene had not escaped the war.

I could see myself enjoying *a quiet, peaceful life here, if the neighbors weren't sure to kill me.*

The setting sun made it harder to see, so I went back up to the roof. The other PSYOP team adjusted their speaker from behind the cover of a corner of a building to point across the bridge.

Entibah, Entibah!

The speaker crackled to life, commanding, "Attention, Attention!" in Arabic.

Curious faces peered out from windows across the street to determine what the fuss was about. My Bravo Company comrades broadcast a notice that a curfew would be in effect and that the townspeople should not interfere with the Marines' operations during the night.

Around midnight, an earsplitting rendition of babies crying startled me from my sleep. The intention was to irritate any unseen enemies into showing themselves, but the problem with such harassment broadcasts is that the broadcasters are unable to rest either. I tossed and turned irritably but could not shut out the noise. Just when I had begun to really hate the speaker, the baby's cries were replaced by an even more horrendous loop: mewling cats in heat. If there hadn't been anyone in town who wanted to fight after those two hours of dreadful noise, I'm sure we made more than a few enemies with the racket. I approached the verge of complaining myself before the aural assault finally stopped. But the anticipation of waiting in silence for it to resume without warning proved almost as upsetting.

Any hopes I had for a peaceful night were drowned in a disjointed cacophony of barnyard noises, threats, and insults to our hidden opponents. However, the night passed without any sign of them.

Dawn broke, and mosques across the river responded with their own speakers, echoing the call to prayer. Ali warned that the Imam seemed upset and was calling for the people to stand up to the occupier. I could hear honking from an unseen highway on the other side of the hill.

Then for several hours, all was still. A palpable tension rose in conjunction with the heat. Something was not right. I couldn't justify my feeling, but the quiet did not fit the mood.

Suddenly, the distinctive double *Boom, BOOM!* of rocket-propelled grenades shattered the stillness as their engines burst from their launchers and whooshed across the river to explode against our rooftop redoubt!

Enemy gunners waiting for the signal opened fire with their machine guns from the shadows of the palm grove on the riverbank.

"Incoming!" Cat shouted as he leapt to man the machine gun. I scrambled to join him with my SAW, slamming it atop the retaining wall and sighting down the barrel. Spent cartridges from our guns jingled as they spat upon the rooftop. I heard the careful shots of Marine snipers picking off targets from positions behind us.

My reaction was all muscle memory. I had the distinct sensation of being back on the range where I had zeroed my weapon. It had been a rainy day, and I lay in the mud making adjustments until the gun fired exactly where I aimed. Today, the men on the other side of my finely tuned sights fell as easily as those plastic targets had.

Aim. Squeeze.

The recoil of the gun jogged my shoulder with rapid taps as it spit out stinging rays of metal. With each shot the bipod scratched backward on the lip of the retaining wall. I fired short bursts to compensate, and carefully sighted down the barrel to pivot onto the next target. Without thought, I felt no remorse, seeing the enemy crumple to the ground and knowing that I had just ended a man's life. In the moment, they were only plastic targets, muzzle flashes, and shadows, not human beings. I didn't consider their families or their motivations. I felt no fear, only adrenaline. Time seemed to slow down, so that I could actually watch the bullets glinting in the sun as they sped back and forth over the water. What was only a minute in real time lasted an eternity in the space between life and death. Eventually we realized the enemy had stopped shooting back.

The wind carried faint screams of pain from the palm grove. Cat looked over his shoulder at me.

"You all right?"

"Yeah," I replied, taking a deep breath. "I'm okay. I need more ammo."

I ran downstairs and peeked out the front gate. I would have to cross the street, fully exposed to the bridge, and run to the PSYOP truck for another box of SAW ammo. Hopefully whoever was left on the other side of the river was in no shape to shoot at me. I sprinted across the open space and ducked behind the truck. My mind raced.

Half my mind glowed with excitement. I felt validated as a soldier, having finally experienced combat. The other half doubted whether I would live to see the end of my deployment. It was, after all, only our first mission.

"You guys are bad luck!" Parm called down from his turret. "That's the first time anyone actually shot at us."

Manny conferred with his interpreter inside the truck, crafting a message in response to the attack.

I called up to Parm. "Do you have any extra SAW ammo?"

"There's some in the back."

I opened the hatch, which took some effort because of the spare Humvee tire strapped to it. The pneumatic assist that usually made it easier to lift had been broken by the weight of the tire. I snatched one of the metal boxes of belted ammunition and ran back upstairs. Several more Marines had joined Cat and Josh and were perched behind their rifles, scanning for movement. One of the men was an air force combat controller who carried a radio with a long antenna he could use to speak directly to the pilots of the Marine Corps' F-18 fighter bombers. He conferred with a gunnery sergeant, pointing out buildings on the riverbank. Cat joined them and indicated which ones had been sheltering enemy fighters.

After hours of waiting for a second attack that didn't come, the excitement level abated somewhat. The increasing wind was heavy with sand, which stuck to my sweaty skin. I felt exhausted and dehydrated. Not being able to sleep through the night had left me in a mental fog. I chugged one of the sodas from downstairs and propped myself against a wall to wait for my shift on the gun. Footsteps crunched in the street. I looked over the edge of the roof to see two Marines and one of the lieutenants standing with Ali and an old couple who appeared to be husband and wife.

"They want to feed their cows," Ali explained.

The lieutenant sized up the old man and finally relented to allow the pair into the garden under guard. The big mocha-colored cow munched the pile of dried palm fronds the farmer offered to her quite appreciatively, but the little one kept a safe distance behind Momma.

Huh. I didn't know cows liked palms.

Maybe the old couple was spying on us.

After the owners of the house had gone back to wherever it was they were staying, I intended to ignore such distractions and finally get some rest. I sat down with my eyes closed, face to the sky, and heard a hollow sound at once both unfamiliar and immediately recognizable and terrifying.

Thooomp! Thooomp! Thooomp!

It was the sound of a mortar tube launching death toward us. I opened my eyes in time to see a trail of flame pass directly over my head and land somewhere in the neighborhood beyond.

"Everyone, down!" Someone shouted in a tone of such solemn urgency no one questioned him.

Another mortar sizzled overhead. Another. They were getting closer and the dreadful sound of impacting explosions grew louder. I was petrified by fear. Mortars are called indirect fire weapons because they come from above. The enemy does not need line of sight to kill with them and can launch rounds from behind hills and buildings, unseen. Under an open sky, there is nowhere to hide. I had never felt so vulnerable. Another mortar landed in the alley directly beside our rooftop between two cars, blasting a six-inch hole through the base of a concrete wall and sending shrapnel through our kitchen door. The rear car's radiator fluid bled in a dark circle onto the dust.

The next one will be on the roof.

In that instant I knew I would die, and experienced a strangely peaceful acceptance of my fate. My life was not important, in the scheme of things. I could not change it in these final seconds, and regrets I had were too late. It would be better to go to the wall and die shooting back than lying on my belly, helpless. Sharing the same realization, the rest of our crew converged on the wall and returned an earsplitting barrage of rifle and machine gun fire. The Marine on the machine gun had dropped the plastic butt stock on the ground, cracking it, but the weapon was not too damaged to preclude adding its bass bark to the uproar. We were all so close together and the volume of fire so great that our boots rolled on a brass carpet of spent cartridges.

Josh had a grenade launcher attached to his rifle and very methodically began raining down a hail of high-explosive grenades on the enemy's positions. The first round plopped in the river, but he walked the explosions up the bank with deadly accuracy. Patches of the palm grove smoked and the red glow of fire flickered eerily through the shadow of the trees.

Kaboom!

A rocket exploded against a parapet to my left, sending pebbles skittering across the rooftop. Our opponents were determined to throw everything they had against us. I felt totally free, having already welcomed the certainty of my death. I was no longer afraid. The mortar fire ceased, but I hardly noticed. Somehow it wasn't important anymore.

The other PSYOP team began to broadcast Drowning Pool's *Let the Bodies Hit the Floor* at full volume. The Marine next to me looked over and nodded. He smiled approvingly.

"Everyone, inside! They're gonna shoot the main gun!" yelled the gunnery sergeant.

We crowded into the stairwell. I heard the metal squeaking of treads through the wall as two tanks lurched forward to the end of the street, just outside the front door of our house.

"Open your mouths and cover your ears!" screamed Gunny.

New Testament was back.

What followed was the loudest sound I had ever heard. The pressure wave walloped my chest and simultaneously broke all the windows on both sides of the street with a deafening crash of exploding glass.

"They're doing another one!" Gunny warned.

It felt like our house had been magically transported to the inside of a thundercloud. My ears rang and I touched them to make sure they weren't bleeding, half expecting my fingers to come back red. I could see Gunny motioning for everyone to go back upstairs but his voice sounded far away, as if filtered through cotton.

Back on the rooftop we were greeted by a surreal scene. The assault from the opposite bank had stopped, and the air glowed red with fire, dust and smoke. One of the buildings the enemy had been using as cover from our counterfire lay mostly in ruins, blasted into a pile of bricks by the tank shells. A patchwork of fire ignited by tracer and high-explosive rounds spread quickly through the dry vegetation, and flames licked high above the crown of palm trees.

While we watched, a dust devil materialized out of the west and scoured the length of the grove from the river to the hilltop. The little funnels were not uncommon during the Iraqi spring; we had seen them before. This one, though, preposterously took the form of what could have been seen as a godly disembodied hand, as if to signify the presence of a divine ally. I often doubted the existence of God, but while watching the hand rake the enemy positions in awe I experienced a brief moment of supreme, unwavering faith. Not only had my life been spared in spite of my worst expectations, but I was in the presence of the hand that saved me.

One Marine next to me murmured incredulously. "Holy shit! Do you see that?"

I could only nod my head in grateful admiration.

We had won the day, perhaps with heaven's help, but no one expected the fight to be over. Our watch on the bridge continued. We established a guard roster and I left to find a suitable area to nap until my next shift.

The previous night had been one of the coldest of my life. I always assumed Iraq would be a steamy desert and had left my sleeping bag at the dam, forced to shiver in a corner until dawn as a result. While looking for a better spot, I opened a door and found the room full almost to the ceiling with blankets and pillows! Fleas or not, I slept soundly until startled by gunfire once again. I grabbed my helmet and ran outside but stopped as I realized the shots came from behind the house. It was only the Marines shooting out streetlights to prevent their glow from silhouetting us on the roof. At least, that must have been the reason they gave their boss to convince him to let them do it. From the sound of their laughter they enjoyed their target practice, an activity that would have seen them thrown in jail for vandalism back home.

Josh nudged me awake with the toe of his boot at the end of his shift to let me know it was my turn. The air was cool and still. I tiptoed through the maze of sleeping forms, my path illuminated faintly by a crescent moon. The Marine on duty hunched over the machine gun, peering through his night vision scope.

"Come look at this, dude," he whispered. "Do you see someone moving?"

I switched places with him to see for myself. The Marine shook one of his buddies awake.

"Where?"

"To the left of the bridge, by the water. Do you see someone crawling down there?"

I thought I saw something moving, but I couldn't be sure if it was only his suggestion making me imagine things. Maybe it was just a branch blowing in the wind.

"Yeah, I think so."

Another Marine looked through the scope.

"Yeah, man, I see him!" He whispered excitedly. "Gunny, can we engage?"

The gunnery sergeant walked to the gun and squinted across the river. He motioned for his radio operator and reported the situation to higher headquarters, requesting clarification on the rules of engagement.

"He's not supposed to be out there during curfew. That's a hostile act."

The rooftop and street below buzzed with whispers and the muffled clanking of Marines getting into position to fire, each moving as quietly as possible to maintain an element of surprise. They stood in shadow, shoulder to shoulder against the retaining wall, hunched behind weapons of all sorts, peering into darkness. It seemed like everyone who hadn't fired their weapon in the days before converged on the spot, relishing in blood-lust, eager to exercise their license to kill.

"On my signal," whispered Gunny.

The night erupted in a hell storm of tracer fire and the popcorn snapping of many rifles. Streaking red tracers ricocheted off buildings and zinged high into the sky. Bullets stitched left and right, up and down, toward no particular target, into the town beyond. Some of them were aimed at the car blocking the end of the bridge. My heart soared with the thrill of adrenaline, only to be tempered with disgust. The magnitude of fire felt disproportional at best, murderous at worst, and it still was not clear if it had all been for a wind-blown twig. I stopped firing. I willed myself to stop imagining the scene inside the houses on the crest of the hill as bullets rattled through their windows. Hopefully any innocents who might have been cowering there had already had the sense to flee. As for me, I could say nothing.

Morning arrived quietly, cautiously. The damp stillness of dawn broke in stark contrast to the violence of the night before. No birds sang, and the mosques lay still. Only the faintest roar of a jet circling far overhead filtered through the haze. Smoke still rose in wispy plumes from inside the shadows of the palm grove.

The combat controller's radio crackled with static and a barely audible transmission. He held his sand-stained hand to the earpiece of his headset to hear more clearly.

"Pilot counts thirty-one fresh graves," he said.

The man's eyes were red and puffy from lack of sleep. "And the mortar tube is blown up. They are all dead around it. Must have had a bad round."

The jets he spoke with returned to Barwanah too late to add their bombs to the fight, having been busy with higher-priority operations elsewhere in the country during the night. They had made one pass earlier before leaving to refuel, and I watched in fascination through my night vision goggles as the square reticles of infrared targeting lasers ticked over buildings on the opposite bank. They left without positively identifying any targets. This morning their high-powered optics provided us a damage assessment of what remained of the enemy positions before their noise, too, faded into the distance.

I walked downstairs into the garden. Both cows stood in the corner of their shelter, unworriedly chewing their cuds. The chickens showed no sign of trauma and busily hunted insects, pecking and scratching the dust. There had been no casualties here either, and thankfully the only blood shed on the Marines' part had been that of one young man who tripped running into the house and cut his eye falling onto his rifle scope. Upon inspection of the front of the house, however, the evidence showed how close we and the animals had been to death. The windows in the kitchen were all broken, the floor covered with long splinters of glass. A dusting of pebbles and stucco lay at the base of the outer wall, blasted loose by bullets. Myriad light-colored craters in the stone marked where each had impacted, some only inches below where we had been standing.

I heard barking and turned to see a dog running along the opposite river bank after another who carried something in his mouth. It was light colored, large and awkward for him to carry. Periodically the first dog dropped his prize to get a better grip. His pursuer caught up to him and I could see that they quarreled over a human arm.

I should have been horrified, but watching them fight brought to mind what I had read of Nietzsche's theories in *Beyond Good and Evil*. The dogs did not contemplate how they had come upon their meal, knowing only hunger. Human mores couldn't convince them that eating the remains of a man who might have been their former master shouldn't be done. I, however, felt a pang of conscience. A bitter lump of guilt formed in my throat as I recalled how enthusiastically I had contributed to providing them their food, and how indiscriminately our final nightmarish barrage riddled everything within sight. The darkness, the sense of power, and the fact we fought in a foreign land populated by people who spoke and worshipped in an unfamiliar fashion made us feel unaccountable. In the daylight, things seemed different.

They would have killed me if they had a chance, I reassured myself. *They tried to kill me. I only did my duty as a soldier.*

But the uneasiness remained. Someone cried. I stood stock still, unsure if what I heard carried on the wind was real. Holding my breath, I waited. Again I heard the sound of sobbing, muted and far away.

No. No wind whistling through the trees ever sounded so sad.

Upstairs, the Marine on duty peered through his binoculars toward the village's western edge. Now above the tree line, the sound of wailing women came much more clearly. The guard handed me his glasses and I looked toward a growing crowd of black hijab-clad figures. Some crouched on their haunches, beating their heads with their hands. Others carried white-wrapped bundles I could only assume were bodies toward a series of graves marked by piles of darker-colored earth. Some of the bundles were very small.

Those are children. Or pieces of bodies.

I felt very conspicuous, confronted with the consequences of our night of violence, in plain sight of their surviving relatives. There were children, too, staring into space or hugging their mothers' legs, crying. One by one the black figures lowered the white bundles into their holes and covered them with earth and left. Within an hour the chorus of wails died away and only piles of dark earth and the whispering of the wind remained.

If one could forget the events of the night before, Barwanah might be called beautiful. The Euphrates shone like a jeweled necklace upon the city, her tiny bobbing waves flecked with brilliant spots of sunlight. For six thousand years her waters had borne witness to dozens of changing regimes, been spanned by bridges, and felt her bridges crash into the current. Wars came and peace returned, but the river remained constant. Similarly, the villagers upon her banks inherited the blood of ancestors who inhabited the land before them; before the Americans came, before the British, before the Persians. The same river slaked the thirst of Sumerians, Akkadians, and Babylonians, and fed fields that nourished societies producing some of the world's first writers, scientists, and philosophers. Watching the river, I felt very young. As an American, I had no frame of reference for what it meant to live in a place that had given birth to such ancient nations, each of them built on the foundation of the people and their land. In the shadow of such history my youthful nationalism, based on transient imaginary boundaries, seemed rude and short-sighted.

The layout of the town evoked a sense of tight-knit community with narrow streets and shop windows open to the sidewalk. There weren't any parking meters, but many cars of every make and model parked in the alleys and gated yards. Mosques, not churches, anchored the different districts at regular intervals, their distinctive minarets reaching skyward like so many blue tulips. But behind its shuttered windows, Barwanah seemed not so different from small towns in the States. Arabic signs advertised machine shops and convenience stores, even Korean electronics.

Josh and I walked into a barbershop and grinned to see the matted-haired, dirty-faced reflections staring back at us from a long mirror. The shop looked eerily and only recently vacant, as if the proprietor had stepped out to lunch. Josh picked up an electric trimmer still plugged into the wall and flipped the switch. It buzzed to life.

Josh's eyes lit up mischievously as he asked, "Want to give me a haircut?"

He flopped back in one of the swivel chairs and I draped a nearby filthy towel around his neck. Curls of dark hair left by previous customers still littered the floor. I found a guard, dipped the trimmers in what I hoped was antiseptic solution, and noisily began to shear Josh's pelt of sweat-dark fuzz close to his head. His chestnut hair quickly fell away, revealing a base of untanned skin. I felt safe and happy and trusting of my teammates. Though none of us would say it in so many words, we shared a willingness to die for each other.

As we drove away from town along a palm-lined boulevard, we passed the flock of villagers walking through the outlying fields to return to their houses. The expressions on their faces spoke volumes, though confusing, conflicting volumes. Some turned their backs rather than watch us go. Some stared defiantly and refused to break eye contact, while others hung their heads. A few even smiled. The children though, if their parents did not restrain them, ran beside the trucks with their hands outstretched, shouting,

"Mistah! Mistah! Candy!"

So, too, as had the Sumerians' and Babylonians' before us, 3rd Battalion's control of Barwanah came to an end, at least for the day. The insurgents were sure to be back before nightfall.

We returned to the dam for a few hours of much needed rest and refit, and I took advantage of the opportunity to finally change into a clean uniform. Barwanah's action wasn't meant to have lasted as long as it had, and I hadn't brought a change of clothes. After days of sweating and sleeping in dirt, my trousers were stiff and stinking. I stuffed them into a rubber-lined bag in my rucksack, hoping the smell wouldn't infect the rest of my clean uniforms. Laundry would have to wait. We had already gotten word the next mission would depart soon, leaving just time enough for a quick shower and some hot chow.

The shower only trickled lukewarm water, but I had the fortune to beat the majority of a crush of dirty Marines and treat myself to the unbelievable refreshment of washing the days-old caked grit out of my hair and ears. If I closed my eyes, I could feel almost civilized and normal, imagining getting ready for work at home. I relished the comforting feeling of clean dry socks and a smooth, clean T-shirt against my skin.

Manny and Parm joined us for a final meal together in the dungeon of a chow hall while waiting for a separate convoy back to Al Asad. High walls and sloughing paint enclosed the dark industrial space, disappearing into blackness. The Azerbaijanis stood chow duty, their stern Slavic features enhancing the apocalyptic atmosphere as they sullenly ladled green and orange mush that had once been peas and carrots onto plastic plates.

Manny and Cat went over some final paperwork between mouthfuls to transfer responsibility of the truck and equipment. I tried to make my mind focus on the simple pleasure of sitting and eating. It seemed like we never found any time anymore for quiet reflection, or rest or sleep. We were as transient as the wind.

3. THE ROAD TO AL QA'IM

Our convoy to Baghdadi, a tiny desert town outside Al Asad, in the new-to-us speaker truck proved mercifully unexciting. To avoid mines, those of us trailing the lead vehicle followed as closely as possible the tracks of the vehicles ahead. What few civilian vehicles we encountered on the road stopped and gave a wide berth to our speeding column, a survival habit the Iraqis learned by painful experience over years of occupation. The last Humvee in line wore a sign on its bumper that threatened, *Stay back 100 meters or you will be shot* in both Arabic and English. Each truck alternated the direction of its gun, providing a bristling 360-degree field of fire. If an Iraqi driver failed to slow down, the gunners leveled their machine guns at his windshield and quickly settled the question of who would pull over first. Josh simply followed the other vehicles like a duckling follows its mother, Cat monitored the radio, and I stood upright in the turret, watching the desert miles pass by.

A huge rectangular six-cone speaker mounted in the two o'clock position blocked a quarter of my field of vision from atop the truck. I tested the hand crank at my waist and found the turret swiveled easily left and right on a geared track, an improvement from the old style that had previously required spinning the heavy armor plates by hand. The snaky cable to the amplifier in the trunk twisted around my legs when I turned.

I'll have to watch out for that. I wouldn't want to trap myself.

Parm, or someone before him, had written four or five Arabic phrases
on the back of the chicken plate, an angled piece of armor designed to de-
flect shots aimed at the turret gunner. I sounded out *"Awguf Terra Armee!"*
("Stop or I'll shoot!") and imagined the situation in which I would be
forced to shout the words. Hopefully never. I dug into the compartment
at the base of the speaker and found some bungee cords, matches, and an
empty pack of cigarettes. Another man might have dismissed the find as
garbage, but whenever moving into a new workspace, I'd always been
curious to analyze the artifacts people left behind and enjoyed imagining
their personality from the items they didn't think were important enough
to take with them.

I considered the turret my office. I tried to envision its potential,
cramped though the space was. I could strap my water bottles to the back
of the speaker.

*It's not so rough up here, after all, and manning the gun probably means
I won't have to do a lot of walking.*

I gripped the hand rail with my left hand and tested my stance in the
turret. If I stood upright it felt like surfing over the roadway, but more
comfortable to slide my legs forward and rest my armor on the lip of the
turret to take the weight off my shoulders. I leaned back and scanned the
empty desert. The rushing wind filled my ears as the sun dipped closer to
the horizon.

I could tell instinctively the cluster of buildings ahead would be where
we spent the night even before the convoy slowed to follow a dirt road
toward them. An abandoned school sat a hundred meters off the roadway,
surrounded by a brick-walled courtyard. It made a perfect fortress. From
the second-story rooftop, our sentries could easily spot unannounced
visitors, and the approaches were flat. Like clockwork, the Marines quickly
formed a defensive perimeter around the compound and cleared the buildings. Josh followed the lead vehicle and found we could barely squeeze
through the gate and back the truck snugly up to the wall next to the
others, with not much room to spare.

The classrooms ringed an open courtyard in which Marines burned
the trash from their MRE dinners. Josh and Cat walked the perimeter looking for an unclaimed space on the ground floor, while I helped Ali with
his bags. In every room, jumbled stacks of chairs and desks hinted that no

children had sat in them for a long time. Ali wrote his name in English on the blackboard and erased it. To protect his identity he used a pseudonym. He once told me his name, but after knowing him as Ali for so long, his real name didn't seem to suit him.

Joining him, I wrote, "Welcome back, students" in big letters across the top of the board. Josh smiled and took a break from laying out his sleeping bag to snap my picture while I posed with a stick, pointing to the board as if leading an English class of imaginary students. It was unsettling, sleeping in a school, for its emptiness seemed to my mind evidence of the implosion of social infrastructure Iraq experienced after the invasion.

Where were the students? Where were the teachers? If they were still alive, what did they call a life?

A faint afterglow of dusk filtered through the glassless window, silhouetting a darkening gallery of faceless shapes. I took my boots off and slid under my thin sleeping bag. The trash fire cast long flickering shadows through the doorway, and I strained to make out the labels of the food packets strewn on my lap. I kept a red keychain flashlight in my trouser pocket, but had long since learned to eat and dress in the dark. Sometimes I preferred to. It seemed more intimate, required more skill, to operate in the dark. I'd always had a masochistic streak anyway. Secretly, I enjoyed the challenge of privation and suffering and felt somehow more satisfied whenever I could accomplish anything in the most inconvenient way. Naturally I ate my dinner cold and closed my eyes feeling deliciously deprived.

But suffering is not always enjoyable, I reluctantly admitted to myself in the morning, waking to stiffness in my neck and back from sleeping on the hard concrete floor.

I ran my tongue over my fuzzy teeth and reached for my water bottle. The gray coolness of daybreak brightened the desert and peeked through our window once more. I walked to the sill, spat out a mouthful of tepid water, and brushed aside some petrified scraps of pita bread left there by squatters or former students. Josh stood outside shaving with the aid of one of our truck's side mirrors.

"Everything good to go?" I grunted, clambering over the hood and into the turret to put the machine gun back in place.

"Yepper," he nodded, carefully eyeing the razor he guided over his puffed cheek.

He rinsed the blade with a trickle of bottled water. I would have to grab another case of water soon. In the desert heat, the four of us guzzled at least four bottles a day just for drinking. The stash in the trunk ran through our hands like . . . water.

"All set."

Cat and Ali emerged from the disintegrating huddle of team leaders that had been gathered around a map spread on the hood of one of the other Humvees. They walked toward us.

"Your stuff's in the back," called Josh.

"Thanks, dude."

As we drove, Cat explained the concept of the upcoming mission. While the Marines formed a cordon around the town, our team would patrol to the mayor's house to gauge atmospherics, or the people's reactions to us, in addition to providing a diversion from the search for weapons. It wasn't going to be exciting, but the assessment was nonetheless important because the PSYOP product development headquarters in Ramadi depended on the teams' situation reports of what Iraqis thought of our presence in order to adjust their analyses of each area we covered and to tailor future radio broadcasts and handbills.

When the convoy arrived, we peeled off with the command vehicles and formed a defensive circle at the head of a long street bordered on one side by houses and on the other by a steep rock cliff.

"Good place for an ambush," I remarked darkly.

Although I hope not, with all these kids around.

I could see a cluster of children playing soccer down the street. Josh stayed to guard the truck, ready to drive to us if he heard anything on the radio. Cat, Ali, and I fell in with the column of Marines strolling down the road into Baghdadi. We passed fruit stands selling watermelons, cucumbers, and onions, not far from the fields that grew them.

Only young kids and teenage boys wandered the street, but they seemed receptive and smiled as we walked by. Some flashed thumbs up or greeted us in halting English.

"Hello, mistah!" they cried, eager to show off their knowledge of the language. "What time is it?"

I passed out handbills from the stash in my pants pocket to those I thought could read, and pointed out the phone number their parents should call to report roadside bombs. The younger kids crowded on tiptoes around those who held the handbills, excitedly trying to get a glimpse of the pictures. The older kids basked in their recognition from a stranger and refused to relinquish their handouts, instead reading, or pretending to read, the message aloud to the younger children.

I looked over my shoulder when we had traveled a few dozen yards and saw the same handbills already littering the ground. A middle-aged man in a green Adidas track suit snatched papers away from the kids and gestured angrily for them to go home with a threatening upraised arm, as if to slap them.

Maybe the village hid a darker reality, one less peaceful than it seemed, after all.

My restlessness dissipated slightly upon arrival at the mayor's house. Hidden behind a nondescript gate, the yard flushed green with a well-cared-for lawn dotted by fruit trees. His young daughter dropped the sidewalk chalk she had been happily playing with and hid behind the mayor's legs in the shadow of their house porch. He eyed our crew warily from beneath dark bushy eyebrows and carefully exhaled a stream of smoke from the cigarette he held. With his other hand he smoothed his moustache.

"Asalaam Alaikum," called Ali.

"Alaikum Salaam," replied the mayor dryly.

Cat advised the Marine captain walking with us that we should have Ali ask for permission to enter in accordance with Muslim tradition. Regardless, we would enter, as the meeting had been prearranged by telephone, but we might get more accomplished if we were polite. The mayor consented and welcomed us inside with an open palm held to his side. We followed him into a dimly lit room furnished with rugs and cushions. The mayor's wife hurriedly wrapped her hair in a scarf and scurried into the kitchen to prepare a pot of tea. I noticed a selection of old PSYOP handbills yellowing on one of the side tables.

From the start, our meeting unfolded under a pall of uncomfortable politeness. I sensed the strain on the mayor's lined face as he recounted his village's daily toils. The water made people sick. The school had no teachers. I saw the doubt cloud his eyes as he patiently listened with deference to the promises made that Coalition Forces could help make everything better. He was restless, too. We tried to convince him that as security improved, our focus would shift more toward improving the infrastructure of his town, but we ourselves did not remove our body armor inside the man's house. In his mind, our seemingly innocuous decision implied, *We don't trust you to keep us safe, and we aren't going to help you until you help us first.*

One of the Marines stood guard at the door, as if the mayor were a prisoner receiving his weekly visitors. Some turned down the offer of tea for fear it would make them sick, but the offended mayor tried hard not to show his displeasure.

So presumptuous, these Americans, he must have thought, *but the man holding the gun is always right.*

He smiled and nodded in agreement, but he had heard it all before and still waited for all our predecessors' many promises to bear fruit. We left with his assurance that he would phone the base if ever any insurgent activity disturbed his neighborhood. I doubted he would. If he did, I never heard about it.

We returned to the school feeling rather unaccomplished. Winning these people over would take more time than we imagined. It had been years already. It wasn't surprising given how impermanent we must have seemed to them, and we still couldn't see it in ourselves.

All the major roads in our area of operations were named after various metals and alloys. Other units derived their road names from sports teams, or celebrities, or any topic really, that could be divided into subcategories. According to rumor, somewhere a unit had even named a road after Britney Spears. Route Bronze led back to the dam. Our convoy left the school along it, but instead of continuing straight we veered right onto a dirt track toward the village of Abu Hayat. Ten seconds after making the turn I heard a loud *Bang!* and turned my head to see a spindly mushroom cloud of dust rising thirty feet in the air on the other side of the intersection.

"IED!" One of the rear trucks called over the radio, referencing the acronym used to describe an improvised explosive device, or roadside bomb. My stomach tightened to imagine what the scene might have been if the convoy had gone straight, as the bomber anticipated.

The Marines reacted instantly.

"Find that trigger man!" shouted the convoy commander over his radio.

Four vehicles previously designated as a quick reaction force raced across the field parallel to the explosion, searching for a wire or someone running from the scene. The rest of us pulled off into a herringbone formation, facing alternate directions to defend against a possible follow-up attack from either side. I scanned the humps of dirt in the middle distance with my binoculars but could see nothing unusual.

A report crackled over the radio.

"Victor 6, victor 2 . . . There's no command wire . . . Break . . . Looks like the IED was on a timer . . . Over."

Someone had been watching us. They knew our tactics. The bomber must have calculated how long it took to drive from the school to the intersection, and placed the bomb as he watched us gear up that morning. Fortunately he had been unsuccessful, but it sent a chill down my spine to know our enemy could attack at his leisure and disappear before we even knew he had been there. These men were crafty, not to be underestimated. Our only defense had been luck.

We waited for someone, anyone, to drive by and show interest. The whole village seemed suspect. A second group of Marines walked to the crater to take measurements and pictures of the bits and pieces left of the device. Perhaps a fingerprint or a serial number or particular configuration of parts survived that could implicate whoever had emplaced it.

A white-mustachioed old man soon approached from behind us on a dirt bike, his red-checked *keffiyeh* snapping in the wind. He kept a distance from the road and slowed down as if to indicate his intention to pass through and we need not go through the trouble of stopping him. Maybe he suffered from senility or simple passive aggression, but he could not have chosen a worse time to pass the convoy. Though too far away to hear his voice, I sensed from his body language the distress he felt at being inconvenienced by the inevitable search of his person and his bike. I watched him through the crosshairs of my rifle's telescopic sight and imagined his face opening up and the white fabric of his dishdasha flapping over his prone, lifeless body, stained with blood. Suddenly a tang of bile rose in my throat and I lowered my muzzle, silently scolding myself. The man had done nothing to threaten us, and he probably had not had anything to do with the explosion.

I can't afford to lose my humanity. Not yet. Not when so many already have.

Thoughts of Barwanah still troubled me.

When a search determined there were no more IEDs in the immediate vicinity, our convoy continued into Abu Hayat. The village rested on two levels, one portion surrounded by fields of grain and vegetables and the river, the other perched atop a rocky cliff. With some trepidation, I watched the rough stone wall bordering the edge of the cliff, half expecting to see a hand appear to drop a grenade on my head.

Instead, a tiny child's face—then another—peeked over the edge. Ours was the first force of Marines to return to the village in more than a year, which to our knowledge had not seen any outsiders since. The children excitedly watched our parade of Humvees and tracked vehicles, gradually growing bold enough to show themselves. They sat interestedly on the edge of the wall, swinging their legs and waving shyly. When I waved back, they squealed with delight.

Our trucks fanned out between the scattered palm trees in two concentric semi-circles, facing away from the cliff. Before the last vehicle lurched to a stop, squads of Marines were already disgorging themselves from the open rear hatches of the AAVs, their boots clattering like machinery over each lowered ramp. Marine

The Marines' AAV (amphibious assault vehicle), a cross between tank and steel-plated bathtub, is designed to carry troops from ship to shore and beyond. In Iraq's deserts they serve as armored troop transports and platforms for heavy machine guns and grenade launchers. They are notoriously unreliable when crossing the rough, sandy hills and *wadis*, and riding in them feels like sitting on a paint shaker. To keep water from getting in the engine, the vehicle's designers routed the exhaust port to blow out over the troop compartment. Flaw or not, the exhaust's placement has the perhaps no-so-unintended effect of ensuring that when the Marines arrive at their destination they are half-cooked, high on diesel fumes, and mad as bees.

The farmers who observed us from the fields and farmhouses on our periphery were also angry as they watched the Marines' heavy-tracked vehicles drive through a wire fence and plow deep, jagged ruts into the damp earth of the fields that were their livelihood. One stood with folded arms in the frame of his doorway, expressionless but visibly displeased.

Josh, Cat, and Ali left with a small patrol to search the upper portion of the village for the family of a girl accidentally killed by Coalition Forces a year earlier. I stood alone in the turret, soaking up sun and idly listening to radio traffic. In the palm groves and fields below, the rest of the Marines lined up shoulder to shoulder and combed methodically through the tall grass searching for weapons caches. I noted their finds over the radio.

"Red six, red six, red four . . . Found a 155 . . . Request blast window . . . Over."

"Red four, red six . . . Good copy . . . Battalion confirms your blast window . . . Over."

"Roger . . . Controlled detonation in ten mikes . . . over."

"Detonation in five mikes . . ."

"Stand by for controlled detonation . . ."

A loud explosion echoed off the walls of the canyon. The engineers had discovered an old 155mm artillery shell of the type frequently jerry-rigged by insurgents to make roadside bombs. Rather than move it, they simply attached explosives to it and destroyed it in place.

The sun beat down ferociously. I couldn't touch the metal of the turret without burning my fingers. Sweat ran from under my helmet into my eyes. The bottle strapped to the back of the speaker felt hot to the touch and did little to satisfy my thirst, more like drinking from a thermos of hot tea. I poured some water into my hand and splashed it over my face, tasting the salt on my lips as it quickly evaporated. A pair of pigeons huddled on a shady shelf of the cliff face watched me watch them, with their feathers puffed and mouths open, parched tongues panting.

After discovering several other weapons caches, the main body of Marines walked back to their AAVs lugging flour sacks weighted with rifles and rocket-propelled grenades.

So, it seemed, a deceptive quiet blanketed the valley and hid the intentions of people who hated us but who waited patiently to live and fight another day. As long as they returned the favor we had little choice but to let them wait. Frustration grew, not knowing for sure if the men who watched from a distance were simply farmers or *mujahideen*, but at least they would be short a few weapons next time we met. The Marines filed into their tracks and rumbled back the way they had come, leaving me with a short string of Humvees to await the return of the party from the upper village.

Two young boys, probably thinking we had all gone with the tracks, emerged from the reeds by the river and made a beeline for the path up the cliff. They carried fishing poles and faltered for a second when they realized our trucks were still parked along the road, but continued walking right up to my vehicle.

"Mistah! Give me football!" cried one as he mimed holding a soccer ball.

"*La*," I replied. "*Maku*. No football."

I swept one hand over the other to emphasize the point. My heart had not yet hardened against their pleading childish eyes. I had to give them something.

"Here. Catch."

I tossed down a granola bar to each of them. They caught the treats with great enthusiasm, but upon seeing something behind me ran back toward the village on the cliff, giving up on their attempt to charm any more freebies from me.

I heard the Marines returning before I saw them. A horde of happy children surrounded Ali, laughing and reaching for the candy he and Cat shared. The pair of Pied Pipers descended the path to our truck, waving back to the kids whose grinning faces lined the stone wall. Ali threw a few last handfuls of candy.

"No joy, dude," Cat remarked as he climbed into the passenger seat.

"You didn't find them?" I asked.

"Nope. Nobody knows anything. Typical."

Josh started the truck and we followed the lead vehicle out of the canyon in silence. The heat drained everyone's energy. I looked down to see Ali's glistening forehead lolled back on his seat and his mouth slightly agape.

We spent the rest of the afternoon cooling off in another abandoned school, this one in even worse condition than the last. Most of the rooms seemed to have what looked like petrified human feces in the corners and what remained of the desks were broken and scattered randomly. Piles of childish drawings and textbooks gathered dust against the base of peeling walls. One of the lines in a battered English primer read, "We love Uncle Saddam."

I picked up a stick and jabbed around one room to scare the snakes I feared might be hidden beneath the refuse. With my boot, I carefully pushed aside a sheet of particle board. Instead of snakes, I had the good fortune to uncover a stash of paint and brushes left over from what must have once been an art class. For some unknown reason, in the moment of finding the unexpected, in spite of the less-than-sanitary surroundings, inspiration struck.

What do we have to work with?

I squatted and hefted one of the pint-sized cans to read the label.

Black.

Blackboard paint, in fact. In the dust behind the first sat long-forgotten cans of red, yellow, and green tempera.

The wall beside the door presented a perfect canvas of smooth white plaster. I wasn't sure what to paint, but the biggest can contained the black. That could be the night sky. I pried open the lids of the other cans and looked inside. In all but the black, the oils had risen to the surface and were dotted with colonies of mold.

Nothing a good stir wouldn't fix.

I broke off some splinters of a rotten board and stirred the paint.

First I framed a three-foot-by-four-foot area with a thick black line, and methodically filled in the top half. The paint quickly soaked into the parched plaster and needed a second coat. I painted a range of red mountains, mixing in shades of black for depth and texture. Then grew the grass and the yellow-green leaves of trees and foothills. I forgot the smell of my own filthy body and the oppressive heat. I didn't mind not having blue or white paint. It felt good to create, or vandalize, depending on one's perspective, and the emerging image became a manifestation of the mountains of Montana I wanted so much to see again.

One of the Marines came in and plopped his sleeping bag down.

"What are you doing, painting a mural, Michelangelo?"

"I guess so," I chuckled, and continued adding tree trunks. I stood back to admire my handiwork. Something still seemed absent. To be sure, the river of blood looked a little disconcerting, but without blue a red river had to do.

That wasn't it.
I chipped a flake of plaster from the black sky to reveal the white beneath, improvising a star. I poked out the Big Dipper, and Orion, and remembered the spark of recognition I felt the first time my dad pointed the constellations out to me that winter night in Montana, so long ago.
"You mean I have to go to sleep looking at that?" teased the Marine. He stared at the scene quietly, then crossed his hands behind his head and lay back in his bag, eyes glossing in deep reflection.
I smiled, adding one last touch. Below the grass I wrote in black:

**A gift from the
UNITED STATES OF AMERICA.**

Ironically, as one who might normally sleep until noon if I had the chance, I found it difficult to sleep late the next morning, especially since our operational tempo usually made the time set aside for sleep a luxury rather than routine. With no mission scheduled I certainly had the opportunity, but the extra hours just didn't seem as appealing with nothing except a filthy sleeping bag spread over concrete to call a bed and spiders for bedmates. Rather than staying on the floor daydreaming and sucking up dust, I rolled up my sleeping bag and wandered outside to wash my face and check the progress of my new moustache in the mirror of one of the Humvees.

Under normal circumstances, I didn't grow any sort of facial hair, but with no girls around to make fun, wearing a moustache had developed a novel sort of appeal. I noticed the Iraqis liked it, too, since most Iraqi men wore them. Looking and acting different from the majority of Marines may have singled us out to malevolent observers and our own strict sergeants major, but helped make approaching us more comfortable for a greater number of the ordinary country folk we interacted with.

For some of the same reasons, the HET (human intelligence exploitation team) Marines had started growing their own moustaches, too. Of everyone occupying the temporary stronghold, the Marines of the HET were the only ones preparing to leave the school that morning. Everyone else read, slept, or smoked in the hallways.

The army's TPTs, as well as Marine civil affairs group (CAG) teams, often worked closely with HET, sharing information and intelligence on relevant local issues and personalities. However, instead of intelligence gathering being a secondary capability as it was for PSYOP and CAG, HET actively dragged information out of people who otherwise might never have revealed their secrets. When I asked where they were going, one of the Marines mentioned that an Iraqi man had approached our building shortly after dawn with information about the whereabouts of a suspected local insurgent facilitator. No one seemed to know why the informant had gone out of his way to be so uncharacteristically helpful. Maybe the man had a personal grudge or had seen the suspect on one of our bounty posters. Either way, even if the wanted man had already stepped out of bed he would doubtless soon face a rude awakening.

After watching the HET convoy leave to pluck their suspect from his house, Josh and I leafed absentmindedly through the tattered children's workbooks we found on the floor and compared drawings that depicted Iraqi tanks shooting American planes out of the sky and soldiers marching under flags.

Perspective matters so much to the formation of a child's worldview, I mused. *What we call truth; what we tell our children, is more consensus than fact, and so different from country to country.*

The children responsible for scribbling the scenes of violence and militarism I gripped in my hands had evidently already seen more than their share of suffering. Further digging under a pile of scrap wood uncovered an Iraqi flag stitched together from strips of red, white, and black cloth, hand painted across the middle strip of white with three green stars and the words, as Saddam had written in a declaration of victory on his national flag after the first Gulf War: *Allahu Akbar.* (God is Great.) Josh found an ominous-looking black banner a few feet away. It looked like one of the flags we'd seen in internet videos of Western captives before their beheadings by insurgents.

"Hey, Ali!" he called. "Look at this! What does this thing say?"

Ali held the banner at arm's length and murmured the words to himself. "It's a funeral banner," he declared. "They carried this at the funeral of a martyr last year. It has his name and the date and says he was killed by the Americans. Where did you find this?"

When the HET team returned we learned the man in their custody was the brother of the martyr honored on the banner. Two Marines roughly escorted the blindfolded captive into the room next door, followed by their chief interrogator. The door slammed shut.

Sounds of yelling in Arabic bracketed the slap of skin on skin. Whose, wasn't clear. More yelling. The wall shook as a body forcibly slammed against it. I looked at Josh incredulously and shook my head.

"They don't play, do they?" he said, half-laughing in astonishment at the intensity of the interrogation next door.

We listened uncomfortably to a conspicuous silence. I don't know what information the suspect guarded, but the next time I saw him he sat with his head bowed in the back of a cargo Humvee, still blindfolded with his hands bound behind him. Whatever he knew or had done, he was important enough to take with us back to the dam, and from there on to a proper detention facility, where under the strain of enough time and psychological pressure he might prove less resistant to questioning.

Our convoy arrived atop the dam under an inky blanket of darkness. Maybe it was the fact that we hadn't spent very much time getting to know the place, or maybe it was the unfamiliar top-down perspective, but somehow Josh and I ended up trying to enter on the Azerbaijani side. At first it wasn't clear we had, since the dam was symmetrically constructed and as far as we could remember the staircase looked the same as the one we normally used. It wasn't until we passed a surprised looking Azerbaijani guard holding a Kalashnikov we realized we weren't in the right place. I noticed that behind him all the placards on the doors were written in Cyrillic characters.

"Um, can we get to the American side from here?" I asked, somewhat embarrassed.

He stared blankly back at me, and I realized he didn't understand anything I said except "American." The guard looked hesitant, as if unsure what to do with us, and put a finger up to indicate, "Wait a second." He knocked on the door behind him, not taking his eyes off us. I hoped he wasn't thinking of us as spies or trespassers. Unfortunately, we wore army fatigues instead of the Marines' familiar digital uniforms he normally saw, had just arrived unannounced, and probably looked suspicious as hell to an uninformed sentry. I thought it best to avoid sudden movements, just in case. A tall, shadowy-faced officer answered the door and the guard respectfully asked him something I couldn't understand. His superior nodded and uttered a single word in English, his hand outstretched.

"IDs?"

We handed him our ID cards. For a split second I worried he would confiscate them, but there didn't seem to be any other choice. This sort of thing probably happened on occasion and even if we were in trouble, eventually they would have to escort us to the American side. At least, I hoped so. I dreaded the thought we might have just caused an "incident."

"We must have gotten turned around, sir. Can we get to the American side through here?"

The officer shook his head and returned our ID cards after a cursory glance.

"No, you must go back out and go over the top," he said matter-of-factly, in a thick accent. We thanked him and quickly excused ourselves, before he had a chance to change his mind.

"This can't be right," I muttered.

We stood on a landing high up on the dam, bathed in the pale glow of a full moon just emerging from a break in the clouds. There weren't any stairs leading to the top, only a two-foot-wide sloping buttress I'm sure the dam's architect never intended as a walkway. There were no stairs or handrails. Where it met the landing the ramp stood about three feet tall, while the other side dropped off so far we couldn't see the bottom; maybe into water, or worse, concrete. Either way, at the speed our bodies would fall if we lost our footing, neither possibility was better than the other.

I looked over the edge into endless blackness, envisioning what it must feel like tumbling into it, clawing at empty air.

"I can't believe we are doing this," I remarked to Josh. "I hope they don't shoot us."

I pulled myself onto the edge of the wall, crouched to grip both sides to steady myself, and started carefully walking up. If we hadn't aroused suspicion before, sneaking up the side of the dam in the dark, silhouetted against the moon in unfamiliar uniforms, might have been called a perfect excuse for fratricide at the trial of the Marine who killed us.

"I don't think they'd do that. They've got night vision," quipped Josh. "I just don't want to fall. That'd be too ironic a way to die here."

"Don't slip then."

Josh and I never did mention getting lost to Cat, but he didn't seem to notice, preoccupied instead with making arrangements for transportation back to Al Asad. He had learned from Gerry's emails of another Marine battalion's request for PSYOP support, and as a result, since so few teams were available to support the division, we had been temporarily reassigned to 3rd Battalion, 2nd Marines. It wasn't without a sense of anticipation we readied the truck the next morning. The remainder of our personal gear, ice cream, hot showers, and the big post exchange store waited just a few hours away.

We wandered Al Asad aimlessly for four days doing laundry, watching movies, and visiting the internet café. The PX seemed newly special and our dusty bedroom somehow more luxurious. The base sheltered a safe zone, a welcome oasis of leisure and detachment from the harsh existence just outside its walls.

Our first indication as such came within minutes of turning off the main road toward our trailer, when a military policewoman pulled our Humvee over for speeding. She stepped out of her air-conditioned SUV, straightened her crisp, clean uniform, and proceeded to lecture Josh about safe driving habits, oblivious to the dangers we had so recently escaped. After she left I could only shake my head incredulously.

Priorities certainly depend upon one's perspective.

We were supposed to link up with a weekly resupply convoy to a base called Camp Al Qa'im, which Gerry gravely reiterated as the place a team from the company we replaced had been killed. I knew all too well. Jon, the team's driver, had been a friend of mine. The last time I saw him had been at his going-away party. When I'd gotten the news of his death, I sat at my desk in the battalion operations office, and could only stare at my computer screen holding back tears of shame and disbelief. Disbelief because I couldn't imagine such an animated personality forever stilled; shame because the army had never made me suffer as Jon had. My deployment experiences in Korea had been spent in luxury hotels and nightclubs during the same time Jon sweated in Haiti and gave his life under the Iraqi sun. When I found out about my upcoming deployment to Iraq a few days later, it felt like atonement for the imbalance in the price we had each been asked to pay.

The staging yard stretched bumper to bumper with column after column of semi trucks and Humvees. The civilian trucks had been contracted by a private company called Kellogg, Brown, and Root, which seemed to be involved in providing a large portion of almost every service the military once provided for itself. Their flatbed trailers hauled everything from concrete barriers to prefabricated office buildings. There were water trucks and refrigerated trucks too, driven by a colorfully multinational host of men who sat disinterestedly in their ornately decorated cabs or gathered in cliques by their bumpers. We parked the truck and threaded our way toward the front of the assembly to find the convoy commander. After jotting down our personal information and serial numbers he assigned us a place near the front of the convoy.

Compared to most of the Marines we seemed excessively well-equipped and had one of the few Warlock devices in the group, a black box that supposedly blocked the radio signals used to remotely detonate some roadside bombs. The commander alternated as best he could the military vehicles with guns and Warlocks to keep the unarmed civilians within a protective bubble of firepower and jamming waves.

Slowly, the convoy snaked out the gate toward Al Qa'im on another of the roads named after metals, known as Supply Route Tin. I braced myself as Josh aimed the vehicle down a steep grade. My hips were already bruised from so often hitting the lip of the turret. I glanced back trying to see where the convoy ended, but an endless stream of vehicles still passed through the gate, sun glinting off their windscreens. The small trailer that carried our tough boxes and extra gear bounced crazily from side to side over the rocky ground, leveling out as we followed the lead vehicle up an embankment onto the paved surface of Route Tin. I leaned back for what the convoy commander said would be a two-hour drive.

"All victors, convoy commander, be advised, break . . ." warned the radio. Cat turned up the speaker.

"The bridge we are about to cross is a known IED emplacement area . . . Break . . . Route clearance teams went through here yesterday, but tell your gunners to keep an eye out. Over."

I could see the bridge he mentioned, a plain, two-lane concrete slab that crossed a deep gully and emerged into a canyon edged on both sides by steep walls. Our vehicles slowed to a crawl while the lead vehicle's gunner scanned the span with his rifle's scope. I peered through my binoculars.

The right lane had been blasted away and bits of reinforcing rebar poked through what was left of the road surface. What should have been smooth and flat was instead defaced by a jagged crater, the aftermath of a powerful IED.

"Uhhh . . . as you were. We are going to pass this thing up," crackled the voice on the speaker.

The lead vehicle edged into the gully to follow a winding dirt trail that came back out on the other side of the bridge. I thought I saw something ominous and black hanging on the underside of the bridge. Then it was gone.

Probably just my imagination.

Then again, there must have been a reason the convoy commander hadn't wanted to drive over the bridge, either.

Once on the other side, the road smoothed out. I noticed the engineers had been patching potholes, leaving their signature paint markings and stamps over the fresh concrete as a tamper-evident seal should any insurgents try to bury explosives in the holes. The black ribbon of road stretched unbent to the horizon, smooth and shining. It had been softened by the sun and gave slightly under the weight of our tires. I watched the faint tracks of the truck in front of me and wondered how long it would take to cook an egg on the blacktop.

There wasn't much to look at otherwise, only the odd shepherd boy and his flock or a tent far off in the desert.

Nothing to hide behind out here.

The breeze felt good. I could actually breathe freely for once. Ordinarily, whenever we went off-road the trucks in front kicked up so much fine dust into the air I choked for breath through my neck gaiter. It was pleasant to sail along and enjoy the scenery without dirt caking onto my sweaty face and hands or settling into the deepest crevices of my lungs.

We approached a stone tower that could have been hundreds of years old, guarding a hilltop in the middle distance. The convoy slowed and then stopped. More unpatched potholes waited ahead, along with signs that dirt had been swept from around them to conceal digging. I watched curiously as a Marine from the lead vehicle opened his door and jogged to the first pothole. He peered down into the hole and vigorously kicked away a layer of dirt with the toe of his boot.

Cat laughed in disbelief. "He's kicking it?"

Suddenly the Marine stopped kicking and knelt at the edge of the hole. He took a knife from his belt and carefully probed the dirt, sweeping with his hand to reveal a dull metal circle about eight inches in diameter. He'd found a landmine.

The Marine motioned to his truck for another of his buddies to help him. Together, they gingerly lifted the mine out of the hole, only to reveal another. This time it was the buddy's turn to extract the mine. Both men carried their deadly finds about fifty yards off the side of the road and set them down gingerly. The second man ran back to his truck and returned with a small shovel, some empty sandbags, and a wooden toolbox. He set the toolbox down and began filling sandbags while his partner rummaged through the box. The first Marine placed both mines into the hole the second had dug, capping them with a C4 plastic-explosive charge, and both smothered the pit with sandbags. They jogged back to their vehicle and the call came over the radio for our vehicles to back up to a safer distance. A loud *Boom* followed by a rising pillar of gray dust signaled the C4 had done its job.

At a snail's pace, the vehicles moved forward once more until we encountered another unpaved patch of dirt. The Marine who had dug up the first mine led the convoy on foot now, knife in hand, keeping a careful watch for anything out of the ordinary. The first time he wandered an inch off track, Cat loudly warned Josh to follow exactly in the tracks of the vehicle ahead and we crept forward by inches. No cooling breeze offered any relief at this speed. We moved too slowly to outpace the sand flies, which began to bite at my neck and hands. I irritably crushed their tiny sand-colored bodies between my fingers, and couldn't help but think of the pictures of oozing leishmaniasis boils from their bites shown at one of the mandatory predeployment briefings in the basement of the base hospital back home.

Our guide held up a fist, commanding the convoy to stop. He knelt and scrabbled in the dirt covering a large pothole, uncovering another double stack of mines.

"Oh, great," remarked Cat wryly. "This is going to take all day. Two hours, my ass."

"At least they are finding them before we roll over them," I remarked.

"Yeah . . . you've got a point."

The mines had been emplaced with impressive ingenuity. They hid in a cone-shaped hole of tamped earth designed to direct the force of their blast upwards, amplifying it. Additionally, they lay buried upside down, so that one vehicle might drive over and press the mines further into the hole but not detonate them. Subsequent vehicles following in the tracks of the first thus assumed the route was clear and exploded the mines when their downward facing plungers pressed against the bottom of the hole and activated their detonators. Mines required no traceable command wire and emitted no radio waves that could be jammed. Simply put, they were set-and-forget weapons. Whoever put them there was clever. He was free to fight at his own pace, concurrently forcing our operations to a grinding halt without even having to watch.

After the seventh set of mines had been cleared and destroyed, the convoy commander made the decision to forego the road and head overland to Al Qa'im through the open desert.

The decision came too late to save one of the KBR semi trucks, which found one of the mines the clearers missed. We had been progressing at the relatively rapid pace of ten miles per hour when I heard a muffled *Bang!* and turned back to see a greasy black string of smoke rising on the horizon toward the tail end of the convoy. I later learned the driver escaped unharmed, thanks to his perch high above the roadway, but the destroyed truck had to be abandoned.

Seven hours later, at midnight, we finally drove through the gates of Camp Al Qa'im.

4. POWERPOINT AND PURPLE HEARTS

Our quarters in the new camp were by no means lavish, but they were comfortable. Three of us shared half a building with a Marine civil affairs team, who themselves did not take up much space, so there was plenty of room to stretch out. The plywood structure covered an area about six meters wide and twenty-four meters long, with a central living space furnished with a television and shelves full of toiletries and magazines. Known as SEA huts, or Southeast Asia huts, the buildings were cheap and quick to construct in a simple style popular with the military since Vietnam. Outside, the building's white paint reflected the sun and some dusty tarps draped over the peaked roof kept the rare rain showers out. Similarly constructed buildings along a central walkway housed a post office and small post exchange. Some resourceful residents of a neighboring barracks had built a patio from tank treads and a couch from sandbags.

The most interesting aspect of Al Qa'im was that the camp had been set up inside an abandoned train station. Railroad tracks still ran unused through the middle of camp, the empty hulks of giant grain cars that once passed over them parked where they'd been dropped years ago. The massive bays of the locomotive maintenance building housed a motor pool where blown-up Humvees were patched together or scavenged for parts.

One of the passenger cars had been converted into a small chapel called the "Soul Train." Inside I found only a table and a few rows of plastic lawn

chairs, but walking inside, I felt very peaceful. I hadn't attended any
religious services for a long time, yet I was reminded by the Spartan
surroundings how little a building matters to one's faith. The peaceful
atmosphere made me want to be more thankful for the things I did have:
eyes to experience the beauty of a desert sunrise, an Iridium satellite phone
to call my family whenever I wanted, and friends I would die for . . . if I
had to. Life seemed more precious since I'd realized how fragile and transient it could be.

I wandered around the camp enjoying the coolness of morning, trying
to get a feel of where to find the all-important internet café, showers, and
chow hall. Fortunately all three were within walking distance of the hut.
The internet café was dark and cramped, filled with benches of Marines
cradling their rifles and waiting their turn at one of the few laptop kiosks
glowing along the walls. I took a number from the front desk and joined
in their game of "musical bench," sliding down to make room for the next
man as stations opened up.

When I got to my station, I was dismayed to find several keys vacant
from the keyboard. Evidently the vandals who'd covered the desk in graffiti
liked to pick apart the equipment, too. Luckily I found that if I pressed
hard enough on the nub where the keys had been I could type most of the
missing letters. I logged into my email and waited for the page to load.
The connection was so slow that by the time I'd finished half an email, my
twenty minutes had expired, and I walked out mildly frustrated at having
stayed so long and accomplished nothing.

I'll have to prewrite my emails and save them on a thumb drive, I reluctantly surmised, shaking my head as I walked back to the hut to see if Cat
needed any help with his capabilities brief.

A good brief to the commander, we'd learned from the stories told by
our compatriots returning from the war, could make or break a TPT when
integrating with their supported unit. We needed to be sure we made a
good first impression and let the commander know exactly what PSYOP
could accomplish and the applications in which we were most effective. I
stepped through the door of the hut. Cat hunched over his laptop, his
forehead furrowed in concentration.

"Take a look at this, man. Tell me what you think."

We were all familiar with the presentation, having rehearsed it together back home, but Cat wanted it to be perfect. I couldn't imagine that with his outgoing personality he was nervous about briefing the battalion commander, but I didn't see anything wrong with the PowerPoint, either.

"Looks good. Do you want to run through it one time?"

Lieutenant Colonel Dooney had the furrowed brow of an overworked man. A moustache flecked with gray underlined the battalion commander's gaunt features. He looked up from a desk covered in paperwork to welcome us into his small office. The battalion sergeant major stood next to him. In a gruff voice, he commanded, "Show us what you got, PSYOPs." His bald head and stocky features gave the impression he might once have been a wrestler.

Cat gestured toward the screen of the laptop I placed on a small table in front of them.

"Sir, I'd like to introduce my team and give you a brief overview of our capabilities as a tactical PSYOP team and some suggestions how we might best help achieve your intent."

Colonel Dooney nodded slightly and greeted us politely, if humorlessly, as Cat introduced Josh and me.

Cat clicked through the slides as he discussed the limitations and advantages of our speaker truck and how our team could help not only induce surrender of the enemy, but also be employed in crowd control and tactical deception or harassment operations. He spoke briefly about our weapons systems and the disadvantages of a long approval process for new handbills and the distant location of our product development detachment in Ramadi.

"We are not just leaflets and loudspeakers, sir, although we certainly have that capability. We are trained to provide both lethal and nonlethal fires to positively influence the audiences in your area of operations and counter enemy disinformation. We are, sir, simply put, a conduit for your voice to be heard on the battlefield."

The colonel eyed Cat thoughtfully. "Very nice, Sergeant. We can certainly use you. I hope you are ready to hit the ground running. Get with Major Knight. I think he has something for you."

Major Knight was the battalion operations officer, one of the commander's most trusted aides. We walked down the hall to the operations center to see if we could find him. Computers and radios covered every flat surface and maps of the area around the camp reached to every corner. A group of Marines stood around a large projection screen, engrossed in the black-and-white video of an Iraqi town seen from above. It was drone footage, streaming live from a remotely piloted flying robot. I looked around the room for anyone operating a joystick, but didn't see him.

"Is Major Knight around here?" Cat asked.

"In there." One of the Marines in the semicircle indicated with a pointed finger the side office with an open door. "You guys army?"

"Yes, sir," replied Cat. "We're your new TPT."

A cloud of confusion darkened the Marine's face. He didn't understand the acronym. "Are you part of the task force?" he wondered, referring to the Special Forces contingent on the other side of the camp.

"No, sir," I added. "We're PSYOP. That's our speaker truck out front."

"Oh! Well, welcome aboard. We're glad to have you."

"Thank you. Good to be here."

In a service characterized by intense personalities, Major Knight stood out as a soft-spoken and level-headed Marine. Sparks of intelligence glittered in his eyes. He informed us there would be a mission going out to a nearby cement plant the next day, and advised us to talk with Captain Lund, the commander of Kilo Company, one of the Marine infantry companies stationed on the base.

Unlike the major, Captain Lund epitomized intense personality. Even his walk seemed emphatic, determined, and his mannerisms were that of a rushed man with much to do and little time in which to do it. He was conferring with one of his lieutenants over a map in their combination bedroom-office when we found him.

"Basically," he informed us, stabbing at the map with his finger, "our mission will be to make our presence known to the people in the areas surrounding the base, and to gather any intelligence we can while doing so."

Insurgent mortar cells in the towns around us had been targeting the base, and anything we could do to reduce their effectiveness might save American lives. We could expect our operational tempo to be very high because the battalion covered such a huge area with so few troops. Cat dropped off our battle roster information with him and the captain mentioned a time to return for a rehearsal of the mission.

Ali, unfortunately, had not traveled with us to Al Qa'im, leaving us without a translator. After Barwanah he'd decided working with the Americans was too dangerous and stayed in Al Asad to take his paycheck and go home. Cat strode back into the headquarters building to make a deal with civil affairs to borrow one of their translators while Josh and I stocked the truck with water and double-checked that the radios and all our equipment functioned properly.

I liked that the Marines seemed to be visual learners. Planning army operations involves a lot of PowerPoint and paperwork, but the Marines' approach was efficient and direct. When we returned for the rehearsal, a Marine sergeant handed out a single sheet of paper to each of us that included the timeline, objectives, and pertinent radio frequencies of each element participating in the mission. A large terrain model built into a sandbox roughly replicated the countryside surrounding our base with different colored strings and wooden blocks representing roads and buildings. The rehearsal was simple yet professional, and when it was over everyone knew exactly what was supposed to happen, down to the lowest-ranking private.

Still, I felt restless. There is a saying in the army that no plan survives first contact. As I lay in bed thinking about what might go wrong on the next day's mission, I listened uncomfortably to the distant echoes of explosions and gunfire I soon learned was a massive attack on Camp Gannon, a small outpost guarding the Syrian border town of Husaybah, and the impact of rockets on the Haditha dam. They were the sounds of people dying, and Marines earning Purple Hearts.

5. METAL RAIN

S tanding in the turret, I snapped some quick pictures of our small convoy leaving the gate with the hazy industrial towers of the cement factory silhouetted in the distance. The surreal contrast of the vast, cloudless sky and flat, monochromatic desert seemed photogenic in a way that couldn't be captured in a single frame. Many vehicles had taken the same trail before, gradually grinding the sand into a fine powder that billowed in choking clouds from the wheel wells of our vehicles. I put down the camera and pulled my neck gaiter as best I could over my mouth and nose.

One of the shots had been over the barrel of the new fifty-caliber machine gun the Marines in the arms room had been kind enough to let us borrow. My double-fisted grip on the trigger assembly felt solid and reassuring. I felt confident and safe, not only with the added firepower, but because I thought it less likely we would encounter a fight so close to the base. Or perhaps it was a growing kernel of faith in divine protection. Earlier that morning, I'd inked a small crucifix on the inside of the turret with a marker, visible only to me, including the inscription *Jer 1:19*. In the King James version of the Holy Bible, the verse reads:

And they shall fight against thee; but they shall not prevail against thee; for I am with thee, saith the LORD, to deliver thee.

The more I thought about it, the more I believed it. I couldn't explain to myself otherwise why I continued to escape unharmed while everywhere else around me seemed so beset with death and suffering. Maybe God was trying to prove his existence to me. Maybe my faith was the price of his continued protection. As someone who had doubted for a long time, it was a question that gave me more pause than it ever had before.

The plant itself seemed mostly abandoned. The place had a postapocalyptic feel to it, as if cobbled together from spare parts and kept running with duct tape and prayers. Ostensibly the whole apparatus still worked, in spite of its run-down appearance. Most days we could see clouds of dust rising from the towers even from the base, but today the machinery was still. A solitary guard sat at the entryway, looking very fragile and alone. He stood to open the flimsy chain-link gate as we approached, though if he hadn't it probably wouldn't have stood up to a firm push from a bumper. Cat got out of the truck to hand him a handbill with the phone number of the local tips reporting line on it. The man took the paper but gave Cat a look of polite acknowledgment I usually reserve for those who pass out unsolicited religious pamphlets in front of local shopping centers.

After a cursory inspection of the dilapidated equipment by the civil affairs team, the mission was deemed complete. The plant manager was supposed to have met us at his office, but in his absence, we could do nothing but go back the way we came. The major in charge of the civil affairs team tried to reach him on his cell phone but got no answer. A quick search to verify no weapons were hidden in the few corners they could have been and we were back on the road again in time to make it to the chow hall for lunch.

Al Qa'im had started to feel like home. The chow hall always had a wide selection of good food, the Marines seemed willing to let us tag along with a large degree of immunity from the routine pettiness reserved for their privates, and though there were few amenities otherwise, they had real toilets, a gym to occupy our down time, and plenty of missions to keep us busy in the interim.

"If we are going to stay here," Cat reasoned, "we are going to have to get the rest of our stuff from the dam. I'm not going back down Mined Supply Route Tin for a sleeping bag, though. I'm going to see if I can get us a ride on a chopper."

During his routine maintenance the next morning, Josh found that even if we had wanted to drive back down Supply Route Tin and dodge mines, we wouldn't be able to do so in our own truck. The temperamental starter that had been dying slowly over the previous days had finally worn itself out. We unloaded all the ammunition boxes, posters, handbills, soccer balls, radios, MREs, water, and sundry into the SEA hut and towed the dead truck into the maintenance bay next to the long line of other Humvees already waiting for service. It was an inconvenience, to be sure. We couldn't easily move the speaker and amplifier to another truck and the Marines didn't want us welding or drilling into their loaners. To make things worse, we were supposed to support a mission to Ubaydi in two days.

The city of Ubaydi was actually two cities, new and old, with the newer portion supposedly having been built to house the workers of a nearby phosphate plant. Our predecessors in the region, 1st Battalion, 7th Marines, had done their best to clear the insurgency from the area, but since they lacked the manpower to establish a permanent presence, the city had gained a reputation for being a fortified stronghold of insurgent fighters. In the face of this, the loss of our truck meant we would be forced to rely on our backup speaker for broadcasts.

The Man-Portable Loudspeaker System (MPLS) is a speaker in a rucksack with an effective range of under one thousand meters. It is cumbersome, but still provides the ability to broadcast prerecorded messages from the minidisk or amplify the voice of an interpreter. Even with its reduced range, we felt thankful to have at least something to avoid saying, "We can't help you," to the Marines and risk losing the rapport we'd built. Josh may have thought otherwise, though, since he would have to carry it.

On the day of the mission, our truck still inoperable, the only place for the three of us was in the back of one of the AAVs. As we walked up the ramp I chuckled to see that someone had scratched the phrase "If only my girl was this dirty" with their finger into the dust that caked the back of the vehicle. Inside smelled of fuel and sweat. It had the claustrophobic atmosphere of sitting in a boat below the waterline, with no view of the horizon, only the faces of the Marines on the opposite bench staring back. My ears were filled with the clattering of the tracks and the vibrations traveled up my spine into my brain. The top hatch was open and when the transmission shifted, a sickly cloud of black smoke belched into the troop compartment.

There was no point in trying to talk over the racket. I leaned my head back and watched the sky through the open roof hatch. It was gray and getting darker. I wasn't sure if the clouds were really clouds or just dust. It seemed unlikely rain ever fell on this bone-dry corner of Iraq. We stopped and one of the Marines stood on the bench to look outside. I was curious, too. I wriggled around and poked my head out, but there was nothing to see, just the desert and the line of squat, ugly AAVs idling. The wind grew stronger now, and bits of blowing sand stung my cheeks.

The AAV in front of us had broken down. Their gunner leaned out of his turret trying to see assess any damage to the treads, signaling the driver with his upraised left hand. The vehicle lurched forward and stopped. It looked like the treads might slip off their wheels; they'd gone slack. The gunner let loose a string of profanities. He motioned for the track to back up.

"Fuck! Fuck! Fuck!"

The vehicle lurched back and stopped abruptly. Angrily, the gunner clambered out of his turret and jumped to the ground, examining the broken right track.

"Damn it!" he exclaimed, kicking sand at the stalled vehicle. It wasn't going anywhere. Visibility was dropping due to the approaching sandstorm. The only thing clear was that the mission would not go ahead as planned. With much cursing and banging, the Marines attached a tow bar to the disabled AAV and dragged it back to Al Qa'im for repair.

By the time we arrived back at camp the sky had turned red with sun-blotting dust. Gale-force winds bowed the antennas of parked vehicles like blades of grass. I ran inside our hut to grab my camera, hoping to capture the scene, so curiously martian I thought I might never see the like again. The tarp on the roof flapped maniacally and threatened to blow away. When I came back out, some of the Marines who had been riding in the broken AAV stood leaning into the wind, holding their uniform tops open and extended like wings. I snapped the picture and took refuge in my bed, waiting for the storm to pass.

Not until nightfall did the wind abate, and there was no escaping it, inside or out. The sand storm blew in through the cracks of the plywood walls and filled the entire hut with choking dust. We could only laugh about it and shine our flashlights like light sabers though the polluted air. Our faces were grimy but spirits were still high. No one had been looking forward to working or fighting in such weather, and the next day's mission was canceled, too. Our leaders wouldn't risk sending Marines to their deaths if the medical evacuation helicopters couldn't at least see to fly in and pick up their broken bodies. As the walls banged and flexed in the space beside my bed, I heard mercy in the violence of the wind.

When the weather cleared the next day I fully expected to be alerted for another mission to Ubaydi, but the order never came. Our truck had come fresh out of the shop with a new starter and flywheel, so at least the ride to the city would have been more comfortable than on our first attempt. Instead, I busied myself with cleaning weapons and inventorying product, the term we used for our handbills. We'd discovered the key to the shipping container Jon's team once used for storage had been inherited by the civil affairs team, and after popping the lock found stacks of paper-wrapped bricks of handbills still inside. As yet, our own company had not sent anything new. But there wasn't much we could do to change how far we were from their support, and since most of the handbills were generic enough for continued use, the piles seemed a fortunate find.

Tens of thousands of handbills cluttered the container, probably enough to last the rest of the deployment without any addition from the awaited resupply, addressing every topic from proper sanitation measures and vehicle checkpoint procedures to wanted posters of high-value targets. Cat and Josh took advantage of the lull in operations to catch a flight to the dam and back to Al Asad for the rest of their personal gear, leaving me alone to catch up on our random busy work and experience how Marines' priorities change when their focus is off destruction.

In Cat's absence it fell to me to represent our team at the daily battle update briefings, in which the intelligence section shared the latest information on enemy activity and the company commanders outlined their plans for the near future. The main focus centered on coordination for a major offensive they called "Operation Scarecrow."

At the end of the meeting the battalion sergeant major usually chimed in with his pet peeves and told his leaders to *get on it*. His latest frustration was with graffiti in the bathroom stalls.

"I'm tired of seeing that shit," he growled. "You tell your Devil Dogs they can use the Port-a-Shitters until I say otherwise. I'm locking those heads."

I groaned inwardly, being careful not to show disappointment, knowing that as a lowly sergeant I'd be affected by the mass punishment, too. Naturally the toilets in the headquarters used by the staff would be unaffected, but those were already off limits to the lower-ranking Marines, part of strict measures in place across the Marine corps to prevent fraternization between the ranks. Over time, the cumulative effect of such policies had fostered a culture of rank-based elitism markedly more entrenched than I was used to in the army.

Even when I briefed my portion of the information operations slide, I sensed the amusement of several members of the staff at the novelty of a sergeant briefing a room full of field-grade officers and senior noncommissioned officers. Mercifully I performed well enough that they kept their comments to themselves. But regardless of how I felt about it, I had to admit the sergeant major's plan would probably work. In an environment of few luxuries, the graffiti artists would rather give up drawing crude images of genitalia and writing comments about whose unit was better than lose running water for their toothbrushes and air-conditioned toilets.

After sending Cat an email to let him know about the upcoming operation plans and eating dinner by myself, I visited the bathroom to verify the sergeant major's threat. It was locked. A sign taped to the door read, "Closed until further notice by order of the Battalion Command Sergeant Major." The latrines quietly reopened overnight, but by then the sergeant major had made it clear he had the power to make life very uncomfortable.

He did not, however, have anything to do with shutting off our electricity. A few generators provided the only reliable power to the camp, mostly reserved for the headquarters building and the small clinic next to the medivac helipad. Everyone else, including a large portion of the Iraqis in the towns around our camp, relied on power from the Haditha dam's hydroelectric turbines. Brown-outs and black-outs were common whenever the dam's generators were taken offline for maintenance or when demand soared too high. Especially during the hottest days, when people ran their air conditioning the most, electricity was unreliable. On one of these days, when tempers ran high because there was no escape from the heat, I first saw Iraq's rare rain.

I'd found an excuse to stay in the headquarters building and enjoy the air conditioning, though normally I preferred to make my time there as short as possible. Our TPT's workspace was in fact only a borrowed desk in the corner of the information operations office we shared with them and civil affairs. Cat had already gotten into a few pointless arguments with Hart, one of the IO sergeants, which afterward made visiting the office uncomfortable.

Staff Sergeant Hart was the type of man one suspects might have been teased as a child and never lost a desire for revenge. Upon reaching a position of authority, he took sadistic pleasure in embarrassing others and making simple things difficult. I sat at my laptop typing up a report on the day's mission with civil affairs to pay a construction contractor and the broadcast of some noninterference and harassment scripts Colonel Dooney had asked for, listening awkwardly to Hart snipe about Cat to his coworkers. I wasn't sure if he was intentionally trying to bait me, but rather than get involved in another confrontation I stepped outside to cool my head.

Fat, wet blobs of rain splattered with an audible *plop* on the pavement, drying quickly at first. As the pavement cooled their dark wetness pooled together and the rain drops fell faster. I put my hand out to feel the sting of heavy droplets smack my palm. The air was rich with the smell of ozone and the dry, gray leaves of the trees that shaded the interpreters' trailers across the parking lot glowed neon green as their dusty overcoats were washed away.

My mind flashed back to Seoul, and thoughts of running through the monsoon-like rains and flooded streets without an umbrella, happily looking forward to meeting my friends for dinner. My leather shoes had been ruined that day, but I didn't care. It had been a time in my life I felt I would live forever. Yet, Seoul itself had been totally destroyed by war not so long ago and rebuilt from ashes to become one of the ultramodern, glass-and-steel financial capitals of East Asia. Maybe one day Iraq would have the same fortune to rebrand itself as a place of promise, even happiness, where people could forget the evil stain of violence.

But not yet. Not here. That night, lying on my damp mattress, I again heard the drums of war booming in Husaybah.

Left alone, I found the daily routine of life at Al Qa'im lonely and boring with neither regular missions to break the monotony nor my friends Josh and Cat, so I'd agreed to man the gun for one of the civil affairs trucks on an assessment of the phosphate plant outside the tiny village of Akashat. I didn't want to file another "Nothing Significant" report with my head-quarters, and a niggling inner voice of guilt after a few days of lounging in the hooch told me I should get outside the wire to do something pro-ductive.

We stopped in a little orchard, and I found myself wondering again how a land with as much potential as Iraq had become such a terrible place. Dozens of little brown finches hopped happily between the scraggly branches, whistling to each other and interacting the way they do all over the world. The entire scene, in fact, could have been transplanted from anywhere. Surrounding bushes sported a bloom of colorful red-and-pink flowers, sunlight splashed through the shadows less blisteringly hot than usual, and the shade of the trees protected a patchy carpet of emerald grass. A large dry fountain had once chimed in with its merry bubbling, but today it only gathered dust. On the wall behind it someone had chipped off the face of a waist-length portrait of Saddam Hussein done in porcelain tile. The garden would make a good spot for a picnic if only someone could be found to care for it.

Like the cement plant, the complex looked run-down and largely aban-doned. We knew too well, though, the unreliability of first impressions of the absence of danger and kept a sharp lookout as we ascended a short flight of broad concrete steps to the main office. The civil affairs team's major placed a cell-phone call to the foreman, who for security reasons we hadn't told exactly when we were coming, and waited.

We watched him through the thick-paned glass, hustling down a flight of stairs and across the lobby to unlock the doors for us. From outside, the unadorned edifice betrayed no hint of its inner beauty. The lobby and hall-ways were paved with immaculately swept white tile, and the cool draft that greeted our entrance felt like the breath of heaven. It was dark, but the windows let in enough light that we were still able to see clearly. I took off my helmet and breathed deeply. Sweat dried coolly on my temples.

These conversations were always about money. All over the country American millions flowed freely into countless reconstruction projects such as this one, with a minimum of oversight, but finding evidence of results proportional to the huge amounts of cash being spent remained notoriously difficult. From what I could tell, no one really cared. Our budget was without end, as was the list of men willing to take our money. The act of spending in itself was almost more important than to what degree the government was overcharged for goods and labor purchased. We had to offset the destruction done in the name of our flag, to compensate for blood spilt in error with schools and roads. We used aid as a weapon to break the spirit of resistance and prove ourselves the force more capable than our enemy of providing life's necessities, and in doing so hopefully force a sense of obligation from the people to repay us for our kindness with complicity. If we couldn't win their hearts by force of arms, we would buy them.

The foreman wanted more money to rehabilitate the plant, but the civil affairs team wasn't satisfied with the progress he'd made with the money they had already given him. In his own mind, his was the logic of a survivor trapped between two armed camps, willing to take as much as was offered to him from anyone for as long as possible, but we Americans perceived his requests as bordering on embezzlement, or a thinly veiled shakedown, and the frustration showed in the major's face. We left the foreman with the number to our office and made the trip back to camp, arriving just after the chow hall closed.

I put away my armor and sat at my desk to file the day's report. My stomach growled to remind me I hadn't had breakfast, either.

Another day alone in the office.

I hadn't been able to get the internet working to send my report that morning, and hadn't talked to Cat in days. Every time my attempts to phone to the detachment office actually rang through, no one answered on the other end. I assumed some technical difficulty befouled the classified line between Al Qa'im and Al Asad, and when I tried the internet café, I found it locked behind a sign reading, *Minimized.*

Either someone had been killed or the battalion had begun the planning stages of another big mission. Communications blackouts were the Marine operational security folks' way of controlling information flow from the camp, as they didn't want Marines informing outsiders of personnel losses or imminent movement plans before the appropriate military channels had a chance, if they chose to, for fear of leaks somehow reaching the enemy.

Both explanations were equally plausible. In the scattered towns around the camp attacks against Marines increased daily. That afternoon the civil affairs team blustered through the door of our hut chattering about an attack on their convoy in Ubaydi involving two rocket-propelled grenades and machine gun fire. They had been able to outrun the ambush before suffering any casualties, but not before discovering a troubling bit of evidence: a trigger device for an IED activated by signals from the type of walkabout radios the infantry squads used. More were sure to be hidden in the streets.

After lunch I tried again to phone Al Asad. I'd almost reached the door of the headquarters building when a massive *Wha . . . BOOM!* and wave of pressure tore through the air, and I broke into a run.

I ducked my head behind the wall of concrete barriers protecting the front door and rushed inside, crouching instinctively, as if by making myself two inches shorter I could lessen my chances of absorbing the merciless slivers of shrapnel.

Again.

Wha . . . BOOM!

The door rattled in its frame as another wave of overpressure buffeted against it. These were bigger mortars or rockets than usual this time, and close. Twelve inches of reinforced concrete stood between my body and the shards of metal flying outside, but I exchanged blank glances with the Marines taking cover in the lobby beside me as if to acknowledge, "We've hidden as best we can, but a direct hit will probably kill us. Come what may, we accept our fate, but we'd rather it come another day."

Wha . . . Boom!

The sound had become almost too familiar over the past weeks, but still it heralded a feeling of dread terror that gripped my heart and filled my body with a sick tension I did my best to ignore. The windows shivered and I heard the thumping rotors of Cobra attack helicopters launching from their pads to engage the mortar team. Then, all was still. Everyone went back to what they were doing as if nothing had happened. Our friend Death was dearly known to us by now, his arbitrary visits something we indifferently accepted as an ordinary element of our existence. To live in fear would have been no life at all, and though we did not seek Death out, we no longer outwardly trembled at his face.

Apparently the enemy mortar team shared our same disregard for death; despite their close encounter with the Cobras, they attacked again at midnight.

6. A PRICE ON OUR HEADS

E ven if only for a few minutes, driving the battered blue Land Rover was an exercise in simple, remarkable, unadulterated fun, during which I could forget my usual worries. The doors were dented and some of the windows were missing but the well-seasoned engine growled with a smooth confidence, and shifting the manual transmission of the right-hand-drive truck with my left hand soon felt quite natural.

The battalion shared a hodgepodge pool of civilian vehicles for on-base transportation, Suburbans and small Toyota pickups mostly, but to my eye the old Rover seemed most beautiful. I'd borrowed the keys to the time-worn relic of British influence from the first sergeant and now bounced jarringly along a dirt track toward the edge of the airfield. The shocks had worn out years ago, and perhaps airfield was too kind a term for an asphalt road blocked off when necessary by Humvees on either end to allow helicopters to land on it. I scanned the horizon, hoping to catch sight of one bringing my team back to Al Qa'im. They were running late.

I parked, opened my cuffs, and lay back in the driver's seat, soaking up the oppressive heat that beamed through the windshield like a lizard sunning itself on a rock. Al Asad lay to the east, but the chopper pilots often varied their approach to avoid establishing observable patterns the enemy could use to plan an attack. It didn't really matter from which direction or how soon the choppers came, yet I searched the sky impatiently through the windows with shifting eyes.

Minutes later the sun glinted brilliantly off the lead chopper's windows, a point of white, low in the east. There were three in a row, giant cicada-like Marine Corps CH-53 Sea Stallions, rapidly emerging from the heat waves' shimmer and growing larger. I wished I'd brought my camera to capture their landing, a roaring, swooping, well-practiced precision decent into the huge cloud of boiling dust churned up by their rotors.

When the dust cleared I stepped outside and tried to make out the figures that filed from the ramps at the rear of each aircraft. Several civilians walked amid the crowd of Marines, reporters toting camera bags and black helmets, dressed in their uniform khaki pants and polo shirts, looking frazzled. No one ever escaped being sprayed with at least a few drops of hydraulic fluid by the end of these rides. Still, no one I recognized. I began to think maybe Josh and Cat had missed their flight, and then they emerged at the end of the line, carrying a large black box between them. An Iraqi man walked with them, clutching a cloth sack to his chest to keep its contents from being blown away by the choppers' downdraft.

I offered to take one side of the box.

"No, I got it," Cat insisted.

"Good to see you guys . . . hope you are ready to go on a mission tomorrow."

I couldn't resist breaking the news. "We are supposed to go to Jirijib with CA. And the arms room took the fifty cal back."

We had much catching-up to do. All in due time. I could see they were tired. I glanced to the Iraqi man and his dust-covered moustache.

"Hi. I'm Russ."

He shifted his bag to shake my hand, and replied with a slight accent. "I'm Sonny. Nice to meet you. Cat told me about you."

I paused at the rear of the Rover to swing open the doors. "All good things, I hope."

"This is you?" Cat admired, before heaving the box into the back of the truck. "Nice wheels, man."

On the ride to the hut I explained that the battalion had asked for our gun back for use by another truck on a convoy to Camp Gannon. No, Staff Sergeant Hart hadn't been any trouble for me. No new mail had arrived. As we talked, the sense of unease I'd had for the past few days gradually dissipated. Maybe it had been loneliness, or concern for my friends' safety when they were out of my sight, but whatever the feeling, I knew I felt better upon their return.

The next day it was as if the two had never left. We traveled together to Jirijib, a town remarkable for being unremarkable. There didn't seem to be any fear of violence or major infrastructure problems. Streets were clean. One of the houses hosted a wedding party inside a gated courtyard, attended by about twenty carefree men and women of all ages dressed in suits and Western-style dresses in pastel patterns. A late-model black BMW sedan gleamed in the driveway, its owner's pride evident in a carefully waxed finish. The people greeted us warmly with smiles and many even spoke English. Sonny attracted children like moths to a flame and quickly won them over with his happy-go-lucky personality and generosity with a bag of candy. Unlike Ali, he cracked jokes and his seemingly genuine happiness proved infectious.

What is so different here? Where do they get their money? Why are they happy?

It seemed suspicious the residents should be so glad to see us after so many cold receptions from their neighbors, but their eyes verified their enthusiasm to be real. One of them mentioned the groom was a pharmacist from Baghdad. He had just purchased the Bimmer for $5,000. Out of respect for the ceremony we kept our distance, choosing instead to pass regards to the happy couple through the young men who came out to talk to us.

One of them had been watching us from afar. Uneasily, I'd been watching him, too, waiting for him, silently daring him to give a signal to some unseen sniper. As the initial crowd dispersed he approached us furtively, out of sight of the rest of the guests. Sonny translated for him in a low voice.

"He knows something."

The young man glanced at Sonny, as if worried his words might be misinterpreted.

"He says the hospital in Ubaydi has been taken over by terrorists."

The informant nodded gravely, waiting for Sonny to finish, and continued in quiet Arabic. I glanced at Cat and started taking notes. I didn't know the veracity of his claim, but the kid relayed potentially important intelligence information.

What was his motivation? Did he want money? Was he setting a trap for us?

"He saw a sign on the road," continued Sonny. "The terrorists are calling this region the Islamic Republic of Al Qa'im. They have set up checkpoints and are stopping people."

The young man continued and crossed his arms, looking back occasionally at the wedding party, which remained oblivious. Sonny paused before proceeding, his smile gone, considering whether his words might confer guilt upon himself. He touched Cat's arm briefly to emphasize the solemnity of his point.

"They are hunting you. The Irhabis tell the people they will pay $5,000 if they destroy a tank . . . or your speaker truck . . . or me . . . translator. They say I am a traitor. They hear your broadcasts and they want to stop you from talking to the people."

I quietly swallowed a tiny lump in my throat. Cat asked if the kid had a phone. The intelligence section at Al Qa'im would hear everything he had to say and probably compensate him monetarily. We departed as unobtrusively as possible back the way we had come, but I couldn't suppress the subconscious sensation of being watched. In spite of the heat, a shivery chill crept over my skin and the hairs on the back of my neck bristled. Apparently we couldn't depend on anonymity to protect us anymore. The death threat, though a macabre indicator, was at least a measure of effectiveness. Our enemy's posting a bounty seemed a clear admission we were enough of an influence on the villagers that they thought we needed to be stopped.

The weather didn't help alleviate the mood. As we drew nearer to base the sky filled with rarely seen clouds: dark, black, rain-weighted nimbus mountains.

"Oh, shit! My bed is going to be soaked again," I worried aloud.

It rained so seldom we had applied only a slipshod patch to the gaps in the hut's plywood roof since the last time it rained. The sooner we got back, the drier the inside might still be. Maybe I'd even have time to move my bed out from under the leaky parts. A jagged horizontal bolt of lightning crackled and laughed menacingly across the darkening sky.

One of Iraq's spectacular sandstorms: a moving mountain, advances on Al Asad Airbase. For those in its path day will soon turn to night.

Karabilah burns as helicopter gunships strafe the city.

These rocket-propelled grenade launchers were a small portion of the arms and explosives recovered during Operation Spear. Here they are displayed in 3/2's conference room at Camp Al Qa'im.

This memorial to fallen members of the 3rd Battalion, 25th Marines was dedicated at the Battalion's headquarters in Ohio.

THIS MEMORIAL IS IN HONOR
OF THE MARINES AND SAILORS
OF 3RD BATTALION, 25TH MARINES
WHO MADE THE ULTIMATE SACRIFICE IN DEFENSE
OF FREEDOM.

THIS IS HALLOWED GROUND

A view of the Haditha Dam from one of its balconies on the American side.
The opposite is occupied by Azerbaijani forces.

Cat and Josh remain vigilant following the first of several attacks on their position beside the Euphrates River in Barwanah. Note the spent cartridges at their feet. Many more would soon blanket the rooftop.

Top left: The author's view toward enemy positions across Barwanah's pontoon bridge.

Top right: Children of Abu Hayat smile approvingly and flash a universal "thumbs up."

Below left: Josh and the author patronize Barwanah's vacant barber shop.

Below right: The author left this mural for future students in an abandoned school the Marines used as a temporary firebase.

A Gift from the
UNITED STATES of AMERICA

Cat monitors the radio for instructions to move on to the next objective.

Josh enjoys a candy bar during a tactical pause somewhere in the desert outside Al Qa'im.

The author peers through binoculars across the Euphrates, attempting to identify hidden mortar positions. During this operation, Operation Matador, the Marines would cross the river on a floating bridge section used as a raft.

Tactical PSYOP Team 983's vehicle bristles with several types of weapons shown here during a pause in Operation Matador. The six-cone speaker mounted on top has an effective range of nearly two kilometers. TPTs on later deployments soon learned the importance of concealing their speakers, which came to be called "bullet magnets."

The author celebrates the welcome discovery of an operational ice factory with a liberated block of ice. Temperatures in Iraq reached 130 degrees Fahrenheit.

From left to right: the author, Cat, and Josh. Cat holds a captured AK-47 assault rifle.

A Marine convoy halts along heavily mined Main Supply Route Tin in the featureless Anbar desert. The convoy was eventually forced to travel overland to its destination due to the sheer impracticality of clearing the countless strings of mines they encountered. Civilian traffic avoided this notoriously dangerous stretch of road.

A convoy of Humvees approaches the concrete factory located outside Camp Al Qa'im as seen by the author from his vehicle's turret. Note that the speaker has been removed from its mount for repairs. The device strapped to the mount seen at lower right is an infrared strobe. It is visible only through night vision goggles and is used to aid in the identification of friendly vehicles at night.

Top left: "If only my girl was this dirty."

Top right: Here the "gate" of Camp Al Qa'im bears witness to the battle history of the Second Marine Division. The HESCO barriers used to create a low-speed, serpentine entrance to the camp are decorated with reminders of the division's battles: in the foreground are Iwo Jima, Guadalcanal, Tarawa, and Inchon.

Bottom left: Marines based at Camp Al Qa'im prepare to launch Operation Spear. The "WP8" on the lead vehicle's doors and turret indicate it is the eighth of "War Pig" platoon's vehicles.

Bottom right: The tank called "New Testament" enters the outskirts of Barwanah. Note the destroyed buildings in the background and the presence of children.

Top: Engineers utilize a TRAM (tractor rubber tired, articulated steering, multipurpose) to fill HESCO barriers around a checkpoint, outside the town of Hit. *Photo: Corporal Jan M. Bender (USMC), official Marine Corps photo*

Center: A .50-caliber machine gun mounted on a CH-46 Sea Knight with Marine Medium Helicopter Squadron (HMM) 774 points towards the Euphrates River in the Al Anbar Province of Iraq, February 23, 2006. *Photo: Lance Corporal James B. Hoke (USMC), official Marine Corps photo*

Bottom: U.S. Marine combat engineers build a makeshift bunker using HESCO barriers. *Photo: Lance Corporal Ryan Busse (USMC), official Marine Corps photo*

Army PSYOPS in action: Iraqi children greet an American soldier.
Photo: Staff Sergeant Ricky A. Bloom (USA), defense imagery.mil

Students from a primary school located along Main Supply Route (MSR) Bronze near the Al Anbar province town of Hit hold pamphlets warning all Iraqi children not to point any type of weapon at a U.S. or Coalition soldier. *Photo: Sergeant Paul L. Anstine II (USMC), defenseimagery.mil*

Marines from 3rd Battalion, 25th Marines, escort a homeowner to open doors on his property while his home is being searched during Operation Matador, an operation to disrupt one of the main Syrian entry points for foreign insurgents into Iraq. *Photo: Corporal Eric C. Ely (USMC), defenseimagery.mil*

A Marine armed with an M249 squad automatic weapon (SAW) returns fire after receiving incoming sniper fire in the city of Karabilah, Iraq, during Operation Spear, June 17, 2005. *Photo: Corporal Neil A. Sevelius (USMC), defenseimagery.mil*

At a stop along the way to Al Ubaydi, a flank-armored Humvee of 3rd Battalion, 2nd Marine Regiment, displays an American flag during Operation Matador. *Photo: Corporal Neill A. Sevelius (USMC), defenseimagery.mil*

A Marine sights through the scope of a Dragunov sniper rifle, taken in the city of Karabilah, Iraq, June 20, 2005, during Operation Spear. *Photo: Corporal Neil A. Sevelius (USMC), defenseimagery.mil*

U.S. Marines and Iraqi Security Forces soldiers travel in convoy aboard a Mk 23 7-ton 6x6 cargo truck while en route to Karabilah, Iraq, to participate in Operation Spear, June 17, 2005. *Photo: Corporal Neil A. Sevelius (USMC), defenseimagery.mil*

U.S. Marines assigned to 3rd Battalion, 2nd Marine Regiment, patrol the streets with Iraqi Special Forces soldiers, while conducting offensive operations in the city of Karabilah, Iraq, during Operation Spear, June 17, 2005. *Photo: Staff Sergeant Jason D. Becksted (USMC), defenseimagery.mil*

U.S. Army engineers use a few bays of a floating Ribbon Bridge as a ferry to transport Marines from 3rd Battalion, 2nd Marine Regiment and their flank-armored Humvees across the Euphrates River during Operation Matador. *Photo: Corporal Neil A. Sevelius (USMC), defenseimagery.mil*

A homemade rocket launcher utilized by insurgents against Coalition forces during Operation Spear. Marines assigned to 3rd Battalion, 2nd Marine Regiment, discovered the launcher while patrolling in the city of Karabilah, Iraq, during Operation Spear, June 18, 2005. *Photo: Staff Sergeant Jason D. Becksted (USMC), defenseimagery.mil*

Before and after: An up-armored Humvee is shown on May 10, 2005, just days before it was attacked. The vehicle was later struck on the right side by a single-man-driven, forward-loaded, suicide vehicle-born improvised explosive device during combat operations in the streets of Karabilah, Iraq during Operation Matador. Charred and twisted metal are all that remains.
Photo: Staff Sergeant John B. Francis (USMC), official Marine Corps photo

A single pickup-style Humvee waited at the gate, facing our approaching convoy. When we reached them a burly Marine exited and stopped our lead vehicle, leaning into its passenger side window.

"All victors, convoy commander," the radio announced. "Change of plan; we've got a FRAGO. We're going to escort this EOD truck about a click away so they can blow some shit up."

For a reason unknown to us one of the Cobra helicopters had recently jettisoned its payload of Hellfire missiles onto the empty desert outside the base. The explosive ordnance disposal squad wanted to destroy them before they could be salvaged by insurgents, but policy required they have at least a four-vehicle convoy before proceeding beyond the walls of the camp. A puff of dust spurted from beneath the rear tires of the EOD truck as they peeled off into the desert toward a wall of reddish cliffs and the rest of us made the turn to follow.

Something bit my hand. I looked down at a small circle of mud stuck to my skin. Another tiny sphere of mud plinked the roof of the truck.

Rain!

Or, it once could have been, for what fell now were tiny mud balls. The storm had blown so much dust into the air it returned to earth as these misfits of precipitation, though at ground level the air remained clear. After a few seconds the dust washed out and it proceeded to rain properly though intermittently. Clods of mud flew from the wheels of the trucks in front of us as they rolled up the wet top layer of sand, revealing a dry strip beneath. My skin grew clammy as the rain ran down my neck and chest under my armor.

"Dude, we're getting soaked down here! Why don't you put a poncho up?" Cat called, only half-joking.

"Very funny, dick," I retorted, though I did cover the hole between my body and the edge of the turret with a scarf pulled from my storage space under the speaker. An unseen finger poked me in the butt.

"Hey!" I dropped to my haunches inside the cab. "You want to play games? We can play games," I threatened.

Cat laughed. "Whaaat?"

Josh snickered and looked away, pretending innocence. I stood back up in the turret and lightly kicked him in the shoulder.

"I'm watching you."

Meanwhile, the EOD team placed their charge. They ran back to their truck and we all drove to a safe distance to watch the explosion.

"Detonation in five . . . four . . . three . . ."

A brilliant white fireball burst into the air, consumed by a tower of smoke. The visible shockwave stirred in rapidly expanding ripples around the destroyed missile. Seconds later a sharp *boom* reached my ears.

Before I joined the army I would have been more impressed with the fireworks, but, in the shadow of the memory of recent events, the explosion made me cringe a little. Not that I could ever betray my newfound distaste for violence while still part of a warrior culture that seemingly so reveled in it.

As rain and lightning transformed the normally dull gray landscape into a luminous panorama of greens and reds, I felt as though I'd lived in Iraq forever, and that I might never leave.

7. TORTURED STEEL, BITTER TEARS

From the rooftop of our SEA hut in the distance I could see a huge cloud of dust stirred up by an approaching convoy of LAVs (light armored vehicles): low-slung, eight-wheeled, fast-moving troop carriers that sailed effortlessly across the desert. Josh and I were in the process of nailing down what was left of the sun- and weather-beaten tarps that served as added protection against the rain in preparation for more wet weather. We didn't want our belongings soaked while we were away on the biggest mission yet since arriving at Al Qa'im, an operation being called "Raging Matador."

Cat threw another sandbag onto the roof. I caught it and looked around for a loose spot in the tarp and covered the bubble with the sandbag.

"Looks like a lot of armor coming for this operation," I called down to him. "There's a whole convoy of LAVs coming in."

"Yeah," Cat affirmed. "I think there's supposed to be a thousand Marines coming for this shit."

For several days we'd been steadily preparing for Operation Matador, filling backpacks with PSYOP leaflets to be distributed by the different Marine platoons and prerecording loudspeaker broadcasts on the minidisk player. Josh was a perfectionist, but Sonny was obliging, and each take sounded better than the last.

"Pretend you're the mayor," Josh instructed. "Use your man voice."

The chow hall swelled like an overpacked madhouse with all the extra guests, and the parking areas around it swarmed bumper-to-bumper with columns of LAVs and AAVs. In an effort to bolster base defenses, a paper and plywood sign posted in a pile of sand outside decreed that *Every Marine and sailor MUST fill two sand bags before entering the Mess Hall.*

Whoever typed the sign omitted *soldier*, but it didn't seem proper to argue technicalities. Josh, Cat, and I did our part and threw our sandbags on the pallet with the rest of them, which were taken away by a forklift and distributed around camp to build walls around the most vulnerable structures. Increased retaliatory mortar fire was expected following the outset of operations. Hopefully if any did come it would be blunted by the extra protection around our hooches.

All unclassified lines of communication had been minimized until the end of Matador to help maintain the element of surprise and prevent anyone from inadvertently divulging battle plans, though it was unlikely the enemy's spies had missed the huge buildup of forces at Al Qa'im over the past few days. Luckily our team still had the Iridium phone to call home, which we used surreptitiously to avoid making anyone jealous. Every other phone on the camp, internet, and email were strictly forbidden and effectively blocked.

In such an atmosphere of anticipation and restricted communication, it was inevitable that rumors soon replaced verifiable news. Cat heard another of the TPTs from our detachment had arrived at the camp, and wasn't satisfied when I told him it was likely they hadn't until we'd searched the whole base.

"Just go fucking find them!" he fumed.

An hour of searching later Josh and I came back again empty-handed, soaked in sweat, and Cat reluctantly admitted he'd verified the team wouldn't arrive until the next day.

Rivas and Munoz did turn up in the morning with the next convoy, accompanied by a Marine gunner. Normally both of them worked in the detachment headquarters at Al Asad, but with three battalions involved in the operation we needed their help in providing the necessary manpower to ensure our teams wouldn't have to be split up as we ping-ponged between different companies in the ebb and flow of the future battle.

I asked Munoz, a shiny-bald, perpetually cheerful Puerto Rican what he thought of the upcoming mission.

"Anything to get out of the office, man. We were just out with 982 last week; that was good times. Any chance we get, we like to come see you guys."

I had to admit it was nice to see his familiar face. He shared stories and news about the weeks he'd spent with the other teams, some of them about friends I had not had the chance to see since arriving in Iraq.

But we couldn't spare much time for idle chatter. In the evening, the unwelcome thud of impacting mortars announced the insurgents had no intention of letting us amass with impunity in their backyard. Munoz and I huddled under the concrete roof of the engineers' work bay, listening to the echo of explosions that riddled our camp with shrapnel. It wasn't complacency that allayed our fear as we waited patiently for the booms to stop, but rather an acceptance of how expendable our lives were in light of the thousands already killed on both sides, many with surviving children or more important roles than ours in their communities. Two single men with no great plans would not be a loss that would be remembered long except by our mothers . . . and fathers.

A combination of unforeseen delays and ill-timed equipment malfunctions turned what was originally intended to be a departure under cover of darkness into a daytime mission. When at last we left Al Qa'im, it was as part of a hulking armored column carrying a thousand Marines and a few soldiers. Our train of steel snaked through a serpentine arrangement of concrete Jersey barriers at the main gate proudly painted with names of those famous battles upon which 3rd Battalion's "Betio Bastards" had cut their teeth. Guadalcanal. Tarawa. Najaf. The empty barriers at the end stood like blank tombstones and I hoped that before the day ended there wouldn't be any reason to add "Ubaydi" to the list.

We had recently gotten the fifty cal back from the arms room, but compared to the weapons borne by the surrounding vehicles our gun seemed inadequate. Abrams main battle tanks led the way, lumbering under the weight of their massive 120mm main guns. LAVs threatened violence behind spindly 25mm chain guns, and the AAVs carried both .50 caliber machine guns and 40mm automatic grenade launchers. If we were observed, the mere sight of the convoy must have been some deterrent to attack; intimidating both in numbers and the diverse armament brought to bear.

Against whom, *exactly*, this heavy firepower would be used remained unclear. Iraq's conventional army had been destroyed during the invasion several years earlier and, in the absence of a clearly defined enemy, the mindset of what seemed to be a majority of the military was that as long as they'd been deployed to what was called a war, the war had to be fought against *somebody*, even Iraq's civilian population regardless of how low the actual percentage of the population was engaged in armed resistance. It was extremely frustrating that our enemy chose most often to attack with mortars and IEDs; we rarely caught them in the act of attacking us. So, even without clear targets, as long as the attacks continued the certainty that somebody must be punished for them continued as well. We would bring the fight to them in their towns and villages rather than leave the country or let the mortars rain down unchecked upon us in our bases. Our military had been trained as exterminators, not nation-builders, and wanted to fight, anyways. I could hardly have expected otherwise.

From my observation it seemed most Iraqis worried more about providing the next meal for their families in the midst of a destroyed economy than about fighting. Their misfortune arose from the fact that while U.S. forces usually triumphed in direct combat with insurgents, afterwards we withdrew to the safety of our bases. Inevitably, enemy fighters filled the vacuum of our absence the next day, unopposed. Undoubtedly, sometimes they were the same entity, but as a matter of survival the villagers chose complicity with the ever-present Al-Qaeda and militias over well-meaning Americans rather than risk their lives or disfigurement as punishment for their treachery to the insurgents. Most villagers would have preferred to be left alone. Regrettably, our operations seldom took into consideration provisions for evacuating civilians caught in the middle and we never treated their personal property with much respect, which only fostered resentment and bred more enemies. Most often their birthright and unfamiliar customs were their only crimes, living in limbo between two enemies the sentence they served.

While the entire population of Ubaydi would not foolhardily throw themselves against the wall of steel and fire that rolled against them, the entrenched radicals were ready for a fight . When they showed themselves, the Marines itched eagerly to destroy them all.

Show they did, and earlier than expected. As we approached the edge of the city our perimeter security elements took fire almost immediately from hidden snipers and RPG teams. I knew Rivas and Munoz were in the midst of it. The explosion of mortars, rifles, and grenades grew so intense it sounded from a distance like popping popcorn.

Our truck rolled to a stop as part of the security for the command element behind a low sand berm on high ground overlooking the outskirts of town, giving me a panoramic view of the entire city. But even at a distance, we were not ourselves beyond danger. Minutes after we'd pulled into position, a mortar round sailed into the circle we had formed, landing about fifty meters away. The concussion of its detonation rang off the armor of our vehicles. It didn't seem possible we had been pinpointed so soon. I looked at the puff of dust rising from the impact as if an elephant would magically materialize on the spot. Another impact directly behind the commander's AAV convinced us it was no magic. A well-trained, well-hidden mortar team had us bracketed with accurate fire in a deliberate attempt to kill commanders and neutralize the nerve center of the attack. Leaders screamed on the radio in rage and confusion. This wasn't how the operation was supposed to unfold, but we had to react.

A Marine mortar team ran to the spot where the second round had hit and took measurements to trace the point of origin. They slammed their base plate into the ground and began to launch counterfire.

The team leader stood behind his tube, arm extended. His arm dropped.

"Fire!"

The Marine holding a mortar round above the tube released his grip and swiftly bent forward at the waist to save his ears from the concussion while his partner prepared to launch another.

Thoomp.

"Fire!"

Thoomp.

Their well-practiced mechanical movements epitomized military efficiency. Our enemy stopped firing. At the city's eastern edge, the last of the AAVs arrived and joined a long line of armor that raced from one end of the city to the other, raising a huge curtain of dust in a massive display of force, for the insurgents a foretaste of the hell about to storm their streets.

It was a better PSYACT than any we could have made over the loudspeaker. Our headquarters had facilitated a leaflet drop from a C-130 the previous night warning civilians of the impending siege, but the typically condescending message probably only emboldened our opponents. Unlike the reluctant soldiers American forces had encountered during the first Iraq war, Ubaydi's Islamist defenders were hardcore true believers who very seldom surrendered. If they could be influenced at all, it would be through actions, not words.

Then, before the dust had had a chance to settle, the line of tanks turned and thrust into Ubaydi.

As long as the Marines had planned their attack, the *irhabeen* had planned to receive them. Fighters struck from fortified positions and withdrew to others before their victims knew where to return fire. They couldn't rely on numbers, but intimate knowledge of their neighborhoods and carefully positioned weapons caches lent a short-lived advantage against a vastly superior force. It was not long before billowing plumes of black smoke from burning buildings punctuated the skyline. An unbroken echo of machine-gun and cannon- fire filtered back across the berm. I watched as the Marines took the city block by block, and felt quietly useless as I observed from the relative safety of the command post. The radio confirmed the embattled Marines had already begun to suffer casualties.

One warehouse in particular provided the Marines a fearsome challenge. Converging lines of tracer fire pointed to a dark concrete structure that had been converted into an Islamic Alamo where suicidal fighters made their last hopeless stand against the tanks. By now the Marines' F-18 Hornet warplanes and Cobra helicopters joined the fight and bombarded the building with five-hundred pound bombs, whooshing rockets, and long burping bursts of cannon fire. Listening to the running radio reports of the battle I'd counted three Marines killed in action and eight wounded.

The clash of battle still sounded as the first of the AAVs returned with its cargo of shattered flesh. A few Marines dashed from their vehicles toward the ramp of the track as it stopped at an ersatz helicopter landing zone marked with white cloth tape, previously designated as the main casualty collection point. Cat and I ran to see what help we might offer.

What we saw when we reached the track was a shocking reminder of the human cost of war, more so because these helpless, bloody men were young, supposedly invincible Americans. The first casualty lay stripped of all clothing except his underwear, his skin pale and cold. He leaned unconsciously in a sitting position against the shady side of the AAV, legs straight out, head rolled on his shoulder. I couldn't tell if he was alive or dead. The second was definitely dead, wrapped in a green wool military blanket dark with blood. The third lay propped up on his elbows, belly down on a stretcher. A navy corpsman had just finished cutting away the seat of his trousers and taped a bandage to his exposed buttocks.

"What can we do?" yelled Cat.

"Grab this litter! Medivac bird's coming in!"

The corpsman pointed to the approaching Blackhawk helicopter. Cat and I shielded the wounded Marine with our bodies against the blowing sand as the chopper landed. The patient smiled, enjoying his pain medication.

"What happened to you?" Cat asked over the noise of the thumping rotors.

"Grenade fragment in the ass, man. I can't even feel it!"

"Get them on the bird!" The corpsman and another Marine grabbed two handles of the litter while Cat and I took the other two. More Marines followed with more litters. More injured Marines.

"Lift!"

We pushed the stretchers into racks in the bay of the helicopter and shielded our eyes against the blowing sand.

"See you soon, Devil Dogs!" cried the Marine with the shrapnel injury. He waved unsteadily as the aircraft slowly lifted into the air and spirited him away to the rear for treatment.

I silently hoped his wish would not come true. If I saw him, I'd be in the hospital, too. All through the night, more helicopters arrived in a long procession to ferry away more unlucky, broken instruments of their superiors' painfully irrational conviction that the tide of violence might eventually be stemmed by greater violence.

The cities of Ramana and Ubaydi dominated an area known to harbor weapons smugglers and foreign fighters who took advantage of the region's proximity to the largely unguarded Syrian border, network of caves, and

the natural obstacles provided by the Euphrates River. To further impede
the Marines' efforts to reach them the insurgents had destroyed all remaining bridges across the river not already blown up by one side or the other
after years of fighting that were capable of supporting vehicular traffic. Operation Matador's aim was to cross the river and search the villages on the
opposite bank, which hadn't seen an American presence in a very long time.

We needed a bridge. The solution was an army bridge company, engineers whose convoy of flatbed trailers laden with giant sections of floating
roadway could be pieced together to allow LAVs and Humvees to drive
across the river. They'd arrived the day before, but after many hours of
pushing and repositioning the ungainly sections back and forth through
the water, had still not fully bridged the gap. Our timeline stretched further
to the right, and each hour we waited for the bridge to open meant another
hour we gave the unseen enemy to prepare on the other side. Recognizing
that swift action grew rapidly more imperative, someone ordered we should
use one section of bridge as a raft and start to ferry vehicles across. A tiny
force hiding in the tall river grass on the opposite bank to secure the bridge-
head had already come under sporadic mortar fire and seemed in danger
of being killed in plain sight of those of us waiting to cross.

Josh steered into the line of Humvees positioned behind one anchor
section of bridge that led into the water like a boat launch. The vehicle in
front of us drove over it and pulled slowly onto another section held steady
by a small aluminum-hulled boat at the far end, which pushed our im-
promptu raft against the floating bridge section. Once the truck parked in
position, the green camouflage-patterned boat eased away and joined
another on the side of the raft, pushing the whole apparatus slowly to the
opposite bank. As they approached land the boats slowed and maneuvered
the raft into position so the Humvees could drive up the riverbank.

Before we reached land, I could see the grass grew literally greener on
the other side. In fact, the side we crossed from didn't even have grass, only
dust, a few dry weeds, and piles of rubble and random, long-lost rubber
sandals. I enjoyed the gentle motion of our raft over water, admired the
sunlit glint of blunt and iridescent waves, and watched the foamy wake of
the push-boats' motors. I tried to take a picture but my camera had gotten
so much sand blown into it that the zoom lens wouldn't open without
my pulling on it. We hit the opposite bank with a bump. Josh gunned the

engine until the tires found purchase, and we scrambled up the muddy incline.

Well-irrigated fields of wheat and vegetables flanked the dirt road and vanished into infinity. I'd heard Iraq described as part of the Middle East's Fertile Crescent due to its rich soil and capacity for crop production, but had personally seldom seen much to substantiate the claim. Herds of sheep and cows grazed on fresh fields of greenery under the watchful eye of shepherd boys. Most of them smiled and waved at our passing convoy, but with no more excitement than if they were used to seeing us cross the river every day. As more vehicles arrived we pushed further into Ramana. So far, we were fortunate to encounter no resistance; only livestock and curious happy faces, but if our reception seemed anticlimactic, the lack of excitement was welcome. By the end of the day the bridge stretched the full width of the river and the rest of our forces drove safely across.

"What the fuck are we still doing here?"

Cat smacked his fist against the inside of his passenger window with a meaty *thwack*, furious. Our assignment to guard a road to nowhere seemed like a misallocation of resources on the part of our battalion's planners. A PSYOP team should be out talking to people, not sitting at an untraveled checkpoint soaking up sun. I stared into the emptiness at the end of the road. We were in the perimeter security element for the command post again, passing time, accomplishing nothing. Cat had attempted to raise the operations officer on the radio several times already to request a reassignment with one of the maneuver platoons. Now, however, instead of refusing Cat's request, the battalion ops section ignored him. I suspected their reluctance to employ us had something to do with Cat's fractious relationship with the information operations cell. Staff Sergeant Hart and his boss were Marines, after all, whose suggestions to their parent unit carried much more weight than those of a trio of temporarily assigned army NCOs.

"That's it. I'm going to talk to those fuckers." Cat climbed out the door with his rifle and stormed off toward the command vehicle. The ramp of the AAV was down and I could see him gesturing emphatically to someone inside. A few minutes later he returned with a triumphant look on his face.

"Alright. There is supposed to be a group from 3/25 coming through here in about an hour. We are going to convoy with them to Ar Jaramil."

Finally, we were to be reunited with the Marines from the dam, who at least we knew would be willing to let us do more than pull road guard. In our time with them, we'd come to understand that the men of 3/2 Marines held to an unofficial but deeply systemic insistence that every Iraqi be presumed an enemy; an attitude that provoked widespread animosity on the Iraqi side and contributed to the creation of endless new crops of the insurgents the Marines so enjoyed killing. Theirs was a force of teenaged adrenaline junkies trained for war, not keeping peace, and dealing with civilians came unnaturally. Our presence on their patrols meant they had to budget extra time to deal with the locals' everyday problems, which, if unrelated to security, were often viewed as frivolous. Their officers may have publicly denounced such actions if they had known, but in practice no one frowned when Iraqi children were mockingly taught to curse their own country in English, or were tricked into drinking the urine-filled water bottles thrown to them from convoys; no one checked that personal property was not stolen from houses or that every dead man called an insurgent had ever fired a weapon at Americans.

High body counts briefed well as a measure of military effectiveness, but the accuracy of how we labeled the dead was seldom called into question, and the act of killing did little to create real peace. I couldn't understand how some men could take such sadistic pleasure in the sport-shooting of sheep and donkeys that were the peoples' livelihood. I didn't know how they rationalized their treatment of the Iraqis as less than human, or how their leaders could proudly point to the slaughter of Iraqis as an answer to the problem of resistance to occupation, when the resistance was born out of outrage at the slaughter of Iraqis. I could understand, perhaps, that they acted in the name of avenging the loss of their dead friends, but only if I could also admit to myself I was part of an organization that counted men with an almost inexcusable bloodlust among its ranks. When the convoy from 3/25 left the command post, we didn't hesitate to follow.

Ar Jaramil was an undoubtedly poor but proud village. The simple houses were plastered with mud, but well maintained. A happy reception greeted our Humvees as we wove through the narrow streets toward a hill overlooking the village. Even the old, stooped, hijab-clad women smiled. We stopped to talk to some of the local men who had come out of their houses to ascertain what sort of insurgent activity had occurred in the area and where the civil authorities were. One young boy bravely approached our truck and invited us to breakfast. Unfortunately we couldn't risk staying any longer in a strange area for fear of ambush, but compromised by trading him some MREs for a stack of warm, fresh flatbread.

Swapping meals provided a welcome change for both of us. I was tired of eating the same bland packaged meals, and the bread was probably the only meal choice the boy and his family ever had for breakfast. The round and thin white bread tasted slightly sweet. Unlike the portions served to us previously in some of the other villages, it had been toasted to a delicious golden brown instead of being left to burn charcoal black. Iraqis are known for their famously obliging hospitality, but were not above burning the bread as a passive-aggressive finger in the eye of unwanted guests. Josh drove slowly while Cat took advantage of the pause to hang some pro-coalition posters along the wall that bordered the street before the convoy moved on toward the hill.

Friendly though they might have been, experience had taught us smiles often hid weapons and bad intentions. To find the truth the Marines would cordon and search the village, blocking all escape routes and going through house by house looking for contraband. After a quick conference with the Marine commander, we had our approval to begin broadcasting. I aimed the speaker over the rooftops and covered my ears. Cat pushed a button and Sonny's voice thundered into the village.

"*Entibah*! *Entibah*! Attention! Attention!"

A scattering of birds flapped away from their treetop perches, startled by the noise. I could tell it was loud enough because even far away, heads turned toward the speaker. Old men stopped what they were doing and young children ran inside to tell their parents. The recording continued in stern, guttural Arabic:

> People of Ar Jaramil, peace and blessings be upon you! The fight of the Coalition Forces is not against you, but against the terrorist beasts whose bloodthirsty crimes stain the soil of the great nation of Iraq. We are working with your government and Iraqi Security Forces to root out and punish those who use terrorist acts and murderous methods in a vain attempt to stop Iraq from becoming a

free and peaceful nation. The terrorists and their foreign leader, Abu Musab Zarqawi, care only for their own selfish desires. They kill children and dishonor your holy places. Whoever helps the terrorists harms Iraq. Coalition Forces are conducting a search of this village for illegal weapons and terrorists. For your own safety, remain in your homes and stay off of rooftops. Follow the instructions of Coalition Forces and do not approach them unless instructed to do so. Brave people of Iraq, stand with your countrymen and neighbors to help us defeat the terrorist dogs! If you have information about terrorists or illegal weapons, tell Coalition Forces. Long live Iraq!

Foot patrols moved through the streets as the last echoes of our broadcast died into the distance. We repeated it twice more for good measure, then Josh put the truck in gear and we threaded our way back through the village to catch up with the rest of the platoon. They were stopped at the edge of an open field, eyeing a squarish building that stood by itself on the other side in the shade of tall date palms. The expressions on people's faces in their windows on this side of town were markedly less friendly the closer we moved to the river, as if we had crossed a line that separated the half of the village that supported Coalition Forces and the half that hated us.

One of the Marines ahead spoke with an Iraqi man who kept pointing to the building. Our radio explained the man was an informant who warned the Marines that the building was a booby-trapped police station loaded with high explosives. If a trap waited here, the men who set it would not be far away. I kept a nervous lookout from my turret down shadowy side streets and over rooftops.

Approaching from behind us, a pair of tanks clanked past through the narrow street and stopped at the edge of the clearing. Moments later the first tank rocked back from the recoil of an orange tongue of fire bursting from its main gun and the round squarely impacted the suspect building.

The cinder block and concrete structure erupted in a series of explosions that threw chunks of debris high above the trees. Bits of brick rained down for several seconds. Dust and smoke drifted lazily back into the palms.

So, it had been rigged, as the informant said.

Our group moved cautiously forward, knowing the enemy waited for us. If they did not, more traps most certainly did.

The Marines' commanders on the radio debated whether or not they should use the tanks to clear the rest of the village. It looked deserted.

But if I were an Iraqi and heard my police station blasted into nothingness, I would hide too.

Besides, we had just instructed them to stay in their houses. If we employed the tanks, civilians would surely die.

How could we consider repaying uninvolved civilians in such a manner after their warning about the police station?

"Do they really think those houses are empty?" I asked Cat. "Maybe we should do a surrender appeal."

It didn't take much convincing the Marines that we should be allowed to at least try to coax out the inhabitants, given the number of embedded news crews floating around between platoons, even if it was to demand they do the opposite of what we'd asked of them earlier. The existence of booby-traps had changed the situation, and the townspeople needed to be removed from the equation. I had seen a *Fox News* logo on a television camera earlier that morning. If they did a story about dead civilians, the implications could be disastrously embarrassing for our public image. It seemed the Marines were always more humane when reporters followed close behind.

"Okay, TPT, go ahead and see if you can get anyone to come out of there," came the reply. I hastily jotted down a message for Sonny and he translated it onto the next page in my battered notebook.

Cat readied the microphone. "Are you ready man?" He turned over his shoulder to face Sonny. "We're going to do it live."

Sonny read his translation over to himself again and nodded. "I'm ready, man," he confirmed in his slight accent. He cleared his throat and addressed the empty streets.

"Attention! Attention! Your neighborhood is about to be searched by Coalition Forces. If you can hear this message, leave your homes and come to the sound of the loudspeaker. You will not be harmed. Women, bring your children. Men, lift your shirts to show us you have no weapons. Come to the sound of the speaker. You will not be harmed. If you remain in your house, you will be considered hostile."

We waited expectantly, but no one came. I gripped the trigger of my machine gun nervously. Surely they could hear us.

Maybe the residents had already fled, after all.

Then, movement. A gate opened and two tiny black-haired boys no older than six years old, waving pathetic white surrender rags, stepped into the street followed by a stocky woman dressed head to toe in a black hijab. The Marines motioned for her to come forward but she hesitated at the gate, waving for someone inside to follow her. A man in a long grey dishdasha stepped cautiously into the street.

"Stop! *Awguf!*" commanded the Marines. The man stopped with his open palms facing us, outstretched at his sides.

"Lift up your man dress!"

The man raised his hands in the air and turned in a circle.

"No! Lift up your man dress!"

The Marine mimed lifting a dishdasha. The Iraqi man complied, lifting the hem of his garment to expose his underwear and bare chest.

Better to face humiliation than a bullet, he realized.

The Marines escorted the family into a wire enclosure only just set up in the yard of a house behind us. Cat and Sonny stepped out to question the man.

"Ask him where his neighbors are," Cat urged.

The man pointed back to his house.

"Why the hell aren't they coming out? Sonny, man, you got to tell them again!"

I penned a harsher message and handed it down inside the cab. Sonny sighed and began in a darker tone.

"Good people! Coalition Forces are hunting terrorists in this village. This area is about to undergo bombardment. If you remain in your homes you will be killed. Come to the sound of the speaker, and you will not be harmed. For your own safety, evacuate your homes and come to the sound of the speaker. If you remain in your home you will be considered an enemy. Everyone who can hear this message must show themselves or risk death. We will not hurt you if you are innocent, but you must leave your homes. This is your final warning."

Faces appeared in windows. That had done it. Gates unlocked, and men and women of all ages began to walk fearfully, haltingly, toward the holding area. Some of the children cried, holding their mothers' hands and waving white flags of surrender above their tiny heads. Several men walked out with their shirts removed, indicating they had heard the first message. There were more than I had expected to see, about a hundred. The Marines segregated them into two groups; men in the yard behind concertina wire, and women and children in the shade of the house. Cat opened the trunk of our Humvee and took out a case of precious water for them to share amongst themselves. It wasn't enough, but at least they could count themselves lucky to be alive to experience thirst. After the last old woman arrived, the Marines descended on the neighborhood and started kicking in doors and shot-gunning locks. If anyone remained, they would be shown no restraint.

Morning's still-new light woke the exhausted Marines. We prepared to move on to the next village, Selifa. The previous day's search had been largely unproductive, turning up no insurgents and only a few weapons, mainly just the rifles each household was allowed under Iraqi law for protection of their property. A few military-aged men we'd detained temporarily were allowed to return home after questioning to determine whether they had any knowledge of terrorist activities, none of which they admitted. I wondered how many of them really had taken up arms against us before, and simply chose to hide behind their women and children to wait out our siege of the village. If they were hiding something, the women protected them. No one ever seemed to know anything about anything.

Another platoon of Marines arrived from their patrol to join us in their Humvees and AAVs, clanking mechanically in file as the tanks led the way toward the river. Our column approached a T-intersection, turning left to follow the tanks past a row of large, expensive-looking houses.

"This looks like the rich neighborhood," I said in admiration.

Suddenly an awesomely earsplitting explosion shook the earth. I ducked instinctively in the turret, then snapped back to see one of the twenty-six-ton AAVs that had been traveling behind us claw into the ground after being blown into the air by a massive bomb. It was engulfed in flames and a boiling black cloud of smoke issued furiously from the destroyed track. I heard a volley of shots but soon realized it was only the sound of ammunition exploding in the AAV, consumed within the oven it had become. My stomach turned somersaults into my throat. Dazed Marines fell out the back of the wreck. One of them was on fire. Burning ammunition popped erratically, accompanied by a metallic ping of shrapnel caroming inside the smoking hull. There were not enough Marines getting out. My face and hands buzzed sickeningly. Bile burned my throat as I helplessly watched Marines racing to drag the survivors away from the flames and flying bits of debris.

"What the fuck was that?" Cat yelled.

"Um . . . I think one of the tracks hit an IED," I choked. "It's pretty bad."

The rest of the AAVs tore through the fields surrounding the village in a vain attempt to locate a triggerman, but if he'd ever been there, he was already gone.

The Marines had been robbed not only of their friends, but also of their opportunity for vengeance. We could do little else but wait for the medivacs to arrive in stunned silence. The huge, deathly black column of petroleum smoke still pouring from the track's disgusting, warped shell ensured the helicopters would have no trouble finding us.

Frustration filled the faces of the Marines who guarded the entrance to the abandoned school that served as our rudimentary laager. Down the road the wreckage smoldered, no longer an inferno, but still too dangerous to permit retrieval of the remaining bodies trapped inside. An occasional *pop-pop* of exploding rounds proved just how intensely the residual heat glowed.

But we would not, could not leave the dead behind to be scavenged by animals, or to be photographed and put on a terrorist website. As long as it took their baking tomb to cool, the Marines would wait for their fallen comrades. They stared blankly at the dark, twisted metal, or sat on the steps of the school, crying. At the simple memorial service that followed they hugged each other and wiped away tears, resolute in their determination to carry on in honor of the memory of their fallen. I felt like an outsider; hollow, not fully able to share their grief or the personal knowledge of what had made each man worthy of their words of praise and mourning, not fully able to understand why they, of all of us, had arisen in the morning as we all had, only to meet an unexpected and violent end before sunset.

That night we learned as well that Tony, our roommate from the dam, had been one of those killed in the fighting at Ubaydi. My heart ached that these Marines were asked to pay so high a price, while the reasons for their sacrifice often seemed so hard to find. Beneath their helmets and soot-stained faces, their red-rimmed eyes hinted that many of the mourners were still just boys, barely young men. Granted, these were hard-hearted, long-suffering boys, but nonetheless not far removed from childhood, and in their sorrow, reduced to snuffling with lowered heads.

Very few Iraqis dared leave the safety of their houses as evening fell. Those who did briefly step into their yards avoided entering the streets or making eye contact, and offered neither smiles nor waves. On one yard's wall, a line of scrawled graffiti read, *Down with USA* in English. We didn't have any paint left, but Cat covered it as best he could with posters highlighting reconstruction efforts before retiring to the silent sanctuary of the school.

The next afternoon, after some much-needed time for reflection, we continued with our mission, recomposed, leaving the empty, burnt-out shell of the destroyed AAV as a macabre monument to extinguished youth. Though young in body, we survivors grew decades older with each passing day.

An invisible ring of respectful silence surrounded the blast site, but once we moved farther away, the Marines gradually felt freer to talk again. We reached the river and walked resolutely through the streets of Ramana, showing the people our faces and the fact that we would not be deterred by even the most terrible of tragedies. After some time the Marines even began to smile again.

We were constantly hounded by children. The little ones couldn't understand that they did anything more than collect candy, but keeping the children close provided an added element of security. Even the most cold-hearted insurgent would likely hesitate before blowing up a child. At least, we liked to hope so.

These children though, unlike in other areas, seemed merely to tolerate us, not love us. We were to them the bearers of free sweets, nothing more. Their parents were polite but not friendly. One man stood at his gate with hands on his son's shoulders, restraining the boy from joining the rest of the children who crowded around us.

His eyes seemed to say, *This is my home, stranger. I came here before you, and I will remain long after you have gone. For my family's sake, I will not risk fighting you, but neither should you expect any help from me. In a contest of patient endurance, I will win.*

Frustratingly, almost every person we questioned seemed oblivious to the insurgent presence we knew hid just beyond the edge of shadows.

"Everything is fine. No problems," they smiled, tight lipped, and lied through their teeth.

After the patrol we spent the rest of the afternoon waiting by the river. Intelligence from higher headquarters suggested a group of fighters might attempt to escape the area by boat, so we established checkpoints to intercept them and recorded a surrender message to broadcast should they appear. The boats never came. We lounged lazily in a farmhouse next to the water, watching Lebanese music videos on the farmer's satellite television and poking through his belongings.

Searching through the man's collection of photographs and his bedroom's dresser drawers elicited a voyeuristic, even rapacious sensation, and in the midst of my rifling I concurrently hoped no one ever did the same to my own home. The Polaroid scenes from his vacations and pictures of his family humanized the man who fled rather than endure the battle for his neighborhood. Perhaps he waited just out of sight and would return to put his scattered clothes back on their hangers, push the drawers in and straighten the mirror.

The place reminded me of my grandfather's house after his death: vacant, outmoded, yet brimming with layered years of enduring memories. Like my grandfather, the man grew tomatoes and brightened his front yard with a crop of sunflowers. It was a sobering realization that somewhere, every Iraqi hid away similar detritus of their past, the private collections of knickknacks that made them people, all the small and personal nothings that made them more than just citizens of their unfortunate nation.

I wanted to know his name. The Marines called him "Hajji," an Islamic term of respect for someone who has completed the pilgrimage to Mecca, which Americans had co-opted as a slur.

Charged with killing terrorists, an especially difficult task to precisely execute since the delineation between combatant and civilian was not always clear, the military mindset found it easier to hate and blame the faceless collective for all the ills done by a few fringe extremists. Admitting that collective to be composed of the cultural contributions and personal qualities of individuals made killing more difficult. Stopping to discriminate between the benign and deadly often seemed a luxury we could not afford. It was safer to shoot first, take comfort in the fact that preemptive killing stopped both friend and foe, and count all the dead as enemies.

I put the pictures back in the drawer and walked outside with downcast eyes, disenchanted with the futility of war.

If only before rushing to war we could set aside our pride and perceptions of superiority, and invest more effort in improving dialogue; or if dialogue should fail, in neutral arbitration, and possibly save thousands, maybe millions of lives. If only we valued partnership more than patriotism. If only we were more concerned with promoting righteous and neighborly aims, instead of self-serving ones, we might assuage the hatred and resentment with which our enemies view us, and cure the disease of conflict instead of only treating its symptoms. If only we could find it in our hearts to talk to each other, and really listen to what our planet's fellow inhabitants have to say. If only we could find honest compassion for each other instead of forever squabbling like crabs in a bucket.

There was no air conditioning or fan in the house. Cat, Josh, and I agreed we would rather camp in the open next to our truck than sweat ourselves to sleep, so we each spread a sleeping bag in the dirt and shimmied around to nudge the pointier rocks from under our backs. Ordinarily the desert air and our exhaustion from the previous day would have been conducive enough to sound sleep, but the growling of a pack of hungry dogs circling just outside the security perimeter proved too disconcerting. I kept my pistol close, drifting in and out of consciousness, half expecting one of them to lunge from the darkness and sink his teeth into my throat. When morning broke I was tired but grateful to be moving on.

At last our convoy moved east, in the direction of the rising sun, back toward Al Qa'im. We continued along the river and crossed at the pontoon bridge to meet up with the rest of the battalion, leaving the engineers behind to dismantle it. Our armada churned across the open desert, pausing outside a just-waking Ubaydi. White smoke from the morning's cooking fires signaled that at least a few hardy residents still lived to make their breakfast.

After rejoining 3/2, our team detached from the main element to follow a group of AAVs closer to the city.

No response.

We broadcast a message of thanks to the townspeople and proudly declared success in the operation, expecting to take fire, but the town remained still. The line of armor moved forward. From the command post we watched the Marines retake the city within minutes, encountering no resistance. The enemy had had enough, if any lived, and chose to remain quiet until another day. As the tracks returned from the city, Josh prepared to start the truck and follow them back to base.

Click. Click. Click.

"Oh, what the deuce!"

Josh sighed in frustration. Our new starter was dead, again. Cat apologetically radioed the convoy commander to wait for us to hitch our disabled vehicle to the back of a wrecker and he, Josh, Sonny, and I clambered into the back of a seven-ton cargo truck for the ride home. The sun beat down mercilessly. Sitting on the metal bed of the truck was almost unbearably blistering hot, but it was better than walking, and we had hot chow and real beds to look forward to.

I tried to shut out the heat, dust, and noise, closing my eyes and focusing on the forward movement of the truck.

This ride couldn't possibly last forever.

I dipped my head forward, poured some of the sun-warmed water from my bottle down the back of my neck and relished the relief afforded by the coolness of its quick evaporation. I sat trancelike, drawing careful breaths to not take in too much dust, until the convoy slowed. We couldn't see anything over the armor plating, but I recognized the view out the back as being close to the main gate of Al Qa'im. I stood up to watch the AAVs negotiate the concrete obstacles. Their treads flung up pebbles of asphalt as they bit into the road.

A *pop* of gunfire rang out, very close. I ducked my head back down.

Pop! Pow!

The fire sounded too close to have come from an ambush. I looked over at Cat.

Is that some idiot shooting his M16?

I ventured another peek over the cab. The passengers of the flatbed in front of us were getting out of their truck and fleeing along the road. When they reached what they felt was a safe distance, they turned to watch their cargo. It was no ambush or battle-stressed Marine, only a metal shipping container strapped to the flatbed. The temperature inside the box had risen so high the ammunition stored inside began to explode. Rounds continued to burst sporadically until the camp's civilian firefighters arrived with their pump truck to spray the container with water. The firemen stayed to monitor the sizzling container while the rest of us finally filed past it through the gate.

"We just can't get a break, can we?" I quipped.

But we had been fortunate to make it safely back to base, a blessing not forgotten.

The next day the battalion held a memorial service behind the maintenance bay, on raised ground overlooking a desert bathed in the setting sun's soft light. Each fallen Marine stood before us in spirit, represented by a line of empty boots and helmets perched atop downturned rifles stuck into sandbags. The dead men's dog tags swung loosely from the pistol grips. Before them, the rest of the battalion stood quietly in formation, heads bowed.

"Let us not forget these brave young men," began the chaplain, "who made the ultimate sacrifice to advance the cause of freedom."

He asked some selected friends of the fallen to come forward and eulogize their buddies. They did their best to maintain their composure. Most of them shed tears, recalling happier times. But the dead had it easy, resting in eternal peace. It was the living who bore the suffering of loss.

A bugler again blew the mournful strains of "Taps," each note branding itself forever in my mind. We filed past the empty boots, taking a moment to kneel before them each in reverent reflection, and reluctantly returned to our work. We couldn't afford to dwell on those who left us. The survivors needed each other's support more than ever, and we had yet to prove we would not soon join the dead ourselves.

8. A WARNING FROM KARABILAH

The following days we devoted to repairing the truck and cleaning our weapons and equipment. Spare parts were always hard to find, and the mechanics were not pleased to hear we needed what they claimed was their *last* starter. I suspected otherwise. They had always been resourceful enough before to hide an emergency reserve of parts. As we really didn't have any alternative and there were no Marine trucks that needed a starter at the moment, they eventually obliged us.

Although we weren't running missions as often, we kept busy. We had become adrenaline junkies and felt compelled to move constantly. After the truck was fixed we went back up to the roof of our hooch and patched more holes and strengthened our wall of sandbags around the foundation. We organized product in the Conex. I taught a class on the fifty cal to the CA team. If we weren't working we exercised in the gym in an attempt to stimulate the endorphins our bodies craved.

I was actually relieved when word of the next mission came, because it meant I could stop waiting. Anticipation is a dread feeling, and when confined to the base I felt trapped, like living on an island. My entire life existed within the triangle of chow hall, bed, and office. If the missions were potentially deadly, at least they provided a change of scenery.

Our next assignment would be to accompany the civil affairs team on an assessment of local gas stations to determine the state of their facilities and level of complicity in the area's rampant black market fuel trade. Strung along Anbar's long stretches of paved roads the stations were each hubs of their communities and perfect venues to ensure large numbers of people would be exposed to our messages. We could simply tack posters to the fuel pumps and the message would spread itself, provided no one ripped down the posters.

The first facility was not one that would have been recognizable as a gas station in the United States. It was only a small ramshackle building devoid of signage or convenience store knickknacks and a cluster of large, rusty, cylindrical, metal, holding tanks. A rickety-looking framework of pipes and hoses extended from the tanks and provided the means to empty and fill them. The actual customer's pump drew from the top of a fifty-five gallon steel drum.

Perhaps the posters would look better somewhere else.

We walked into the office, a single whitewashed room occupied by a desk, a white plastic lawn chair, and an Iraqi man whose eyes were still puffy from napping. A dirty window looked out at the rusty tanks and our parked trucks. The man stood up and started to say something, but stopped himself as he pursed his lips in an expression that signaled he thought he might be in trouble. He blinked rapidly, uncertain of our purpose. We had surrounded him in a horseshoe formation, and the man looked nervously between our faces and the door behind us. A barely audible sigh of relief escaped his lips when he realized we would not arrest him.

"Saalamu Alaikum."

The CA major greeted the man with a handshake and touched his chest in a sign of respect. He knew a few phrases in Arabic, but Sonny remained close by to translate.

"This is a fine station you have here. Are you the owner?"

The man nodded his head. "I used to have a partner, but he took his family to Syria. I work here alone now. It's not much money, but it is enough, praise Allah."

"We would like to take a look at your equipment and see if there is anything we can do to help you. Do you get a lot of customers here? You have any problems?"

The major looked out the window toward the decrepit tangle of rusted pipes. No traffic had passed along the road since our arrival.

"No. Yes. It's . . . I used to get a delivery of fuel from the government every week, but I have not gotten a delivery in more than two weeks now. And last week, men came and told me they would kill me if I did not give them free fuel. I had to give it to them. I am almost out now. But what can I do?"

He wrung his hands in despair.

The insurgency funded itself thorough a widespread and lucrative variety of illicit business deals; among them drugs, kidnapping, and the black market trade in smuggled or stolen fuel. I'd read reports of fuel tankers disappearing and seen countless fuel drums in the back of pickup trucks on the open road. The unreliability of the government's fuel deliveries meant it was more common to see kids selling gas out of plastic jugs on the median than to see functioning gas stations. Even at the stations, the line of cars attempting to fill up often backed up into the road. The government ministries were themselves bureaucratically inefficient and corrupt, leading to shortfalls in deliveries and poor regulation. With his hand extended, the owner gestured for the Marines to exit and begin their tour of the equipment. "Please, you are welcome to look."

The Marines left, but the man hesitated. He stopped Sonny at the door.

"You are army?" he asked Cat in English, pointing to our uniforms. "Can you help me? The Marines do not let me have a phone. How can I run a business without a phone? The army let me have a phone before. Why not the Marines? I need a phone."

He cocked his head to the side and raised both hands in exasperation.

"Yeah, that doesn't make sense," Cat shrugged. "I'll talk to them about it."

Maybe there was a reason he didn't have a phone, like using it to report convoy movements.

Josh left some posters and stickers for the man to put up around his office, thinking if he did the job himself they would stay up longer. Ironically, they listed a tips line he couldn't call.

Outside there was not much to assess, only what we had seen through the window. The civil affairs team took some pictures and we piled into our trucks to head for the next station.

The second was much larger than the first, with a parking lot full of tractor trailers. A restaurant and store adjoined the office, doing brisk business. There was even a bright sign by the road with a picture of a roast chicken on it. We parked the trucks and walked toward the restaurant while more Humvees blocked the four-way intersection.

The customers inside all turned their heads to stare at us through a large window painted with different dishes the place offered. We opened the door to dead silence. Somewhere in the back a man cleared his throat. A blend of cigarette smoke, sweat, and roast meat scented the room. I took off my helmet and turned to Josh, raised my eyebrows and whispered, "Tough crowd."

The special of the day should have been cold shoulder.

The manager, a balding man in a white apron, emerged from the back wiping his greasy hands on his belly. Flies buzzed over the meat in the display counter.

"Hello," he greeted warily, in English. "May we speak outside? For my customers, you see."

He led us to the shady side of the building and took a pack of cigarettes from under his apron, lighting one and puffing nervously.

While the civil affairs Marines questioned the manager, Josh, Cat and I wandered toward the parking lot where the truckers gathered in front of their cabs. Most of them had noticeably lighter complexions than the locals, though they were tanned and grizzled as any truckers could be expected to be. Sonny pointed to license plates as we crunched through the gravel lot.

"They are Syrians," he remarked.

"Let's talk to this guy." Cat indicated a red-faced man with blue eyes and a curly crop of reddish hair. All the truckers were watching us, trying hard to appear disinterested. The red-faced man stood up from the step of his cab where he had been sitting as we approached. Cat turned his head to Sonny while keeping his eyes on the man.

"Where is he coming from?"

We shook hands with the man and Sonny replied, "He says he is from Damascus. He is hauling a load of Coca-Cola."

The blue-eyed man looked in our eyes and nodded.

This guy could be from Chicago.

Without warning, shots rang out on the road behind us, making everyone jump. I spun around in time to see a white sedan roll slowly to a stop in the ditch next to one of the Humvees. A spider web of bullet holes pierced the windshield. The doors of the Humvee flew open and two Marines exited, pointing their rifles at the civilian vehicle.

They quickly surrounded the car.

"Get out! Get the fuck out!" shouted the Marine on the driver's side, vigorously motioning toward the ground with his rifle.

"Get out now, fucker!"

The driver lifted his hands weakly. A bright trickle of blood ran down his arms. He pushed his door open weakly, and with one hand the Marine grabbed the man by the neck, dragging him facedown onto the ground. His white dishdasha was splattered with red spots of blood. The man whimpered softly in pain.

"Hey, Doc! Get over here!"

The Marine kept his rifle trained on the wounded man while the other peered into the vehicle for hidden weapons or explosives.

"It's clear!"

A navy corpsman jogged up to the wounded man and helped him sit up against the wheel well of his vehicle. Cat and Sonny were close behind.

"Grab me some water, will you?"

The corpsman pointed back to his Humvee and a Marine ran to fetch a case of bottled water.

"Well, why the hell didn't he stop? Ask him!"

Sonny knelt to question the man, who whispered something and dropped his chin again.

Our translator stood and stated, "He says he didn't see you."

The corpsman gingerly cut open the fabric covering the man's chest with a pair of surgical shears. Five small, dark red bullet holes dotted his arms and abdomen. He barely winced as the corpsman washed the blood from his wounds and inspected his back for exit wounds. When Doc had finished applying bandages, he cradled the man's head with one hand and held a bottle of water to his lips with the other.

"He'll live."

I watched Cat and Sonny walk back to our truck. The Marines helped the injured man to his feet and he limped along, supporting himself on their shoulders. Whether they were taking the man to a hospital or his home, I wasn't sure.

"I guess we've worn out our welcome, huh?"

I grabbed one of our Humvee's antennas to pull myself onto the trunk and clambered back into the turret. Shortly after we left, the radio reported the security element still at the truck stop had shot and killed a suicide car-bomb driver.

That dude must have been testing how close they could get.

Or . . .

I didn't want to mention aloud the possibility a second vehicle had never come.

We slept in the open desert, caressed by warm breezes under an unimaginably dense blanket of stars. I didn't need to wrap myself in my sleeping bag for comfort. I tucked it under my head as a pillow and stretched out on the hood of the truck, soaking up the remaining ambient warmth through my back. Sweat greased my toes and I wriggled them in my boots to get some relief from the day's walking, but it was a disgusting, slimy exercise. Still fully clothed, I sat up to remove my damp socks and boots and set them carefully on the roof to keep the bugs out.

Much better.

I closed my eyes and sank into that dreamless sleep known to the exhausted. After what seemed like only minutes it was again time to move on. The Humvees' engines coughed to life and the muffled static of radio checks popped from the vehicles around us.

Our next objective was a water treatment plant along the route back to camp. From where we parked, I couldn't see anything that looked like an office, only the water tanks, buried under cone-shaped piles of sand. The civil affairs Marines drove off to conduct their assessment, leaving us beside the road.

We linked up with a group of Marines to conduct what they called "Snap VCPs," or hasty vehicle check points. The water tanks provided a perfect cover for our vehicles, as we could park behind them and not be seen until it was too late for oncoming traffic to escape. Additionally, Marine observers had a clear view in both directions for miles down the road. Any vehicle passing by could be searched for weapons, or if they attempted to flee, chased down.

But the road was almost empty. Finally a black Opel sedan appeared, oblivious to our presence, hurtling toward our trap at a high rate of speed. One of the Marines ran to pull a strand of razor wire across the road and his buddy maneuvered a Humvee behind it, leveling his machine gun at the approaching car. The Opel slowed to a stop and the team of Marines carefully advanced. The driver wore Western clothes, accompanied by what looked to be his young family: a wife and two daughters. They watched worriedly through the windshield as the Marine crossed the road and asked for their identification cards. A search of the vehicle turned up nothing suspicious. The Marine waved them through and the family cautiously rolled past the Humvee and back onto the road to continue their journey. We waited idly, like spiders in a web, for the next visitor.

Twenty minutes later the glint of sunshine off a window announced another vehicle's approach. This was a gray Hyundai SUV, occupied by three military-aged males. Their nervous expressions and terse whispers to each other as they stopped at the unexpected checkpoint did nothing to alleviate our initial suspicions that something was amiss. The Marine took their identification cards and thumbed the loose laminate on one of them. He leaned in to check the face of each passenger against their card and said something into the radio on his shoulder. The Iraqis eyed the machine gun pointed at their windshield uncomfortably.

The Marine indicated the driver should park his car in a spot off the side of the road marked with coils of razor wire. Their faces fell, but the men said nothing.

"Alright, Hajji, out of the vehicle," ordered the Marine.

He mimed that the men should form a line, shoulder-to-shoulder. While his partner kept watch he patted down each man to check for weapons.

"You can't be drivin' around with no fake IDs, you hear? You know what I'm sayin' to you?"

The Marine cuffed the men's hands behind their backs with strong plastic zip ties and put his boot in the back of their knees to force them to kneel, said a word to his companion, then walked into the shade.

I waited a long time to see what would happen next. Nothing did. The backs of the men's necks grew redder as the sun beat down relentlessly, and they twitched their bound hands and shifted their knees on the rocks awkwardly, trying to avoid provoking their guard. One tried to scratch his neck with his shoulder, only to be shouted down.

"Don't you eyeball me, motherfucker!"

Beneath the black line of his restraints, the hands of the man closest to us were turning purple.

"You think we should talk to those dudes?" I asked Cat.

"Yeah, why not," he sighed. "I don't think we are going anywhere soon. Hey, Sonny, wake up! Let's talk to these detainees."

I grabbed a bottle of water and jogged to catch up with the rest of my team.

"*Mai?*" I asked the kneeling man one of the few Arabic words I knew. "Water?"

His eyes rolled up to look at me under his eyebrows, expressing both surprise and gratitude. He nodded almost imperceptibly. I held the bottle to his chapped lips and he gulped greedily, water spilling down his chin. The man coughed and I took the bottle from his lips.

"More?" I asked.

He shook his head. I poured some water in my hand and splashed it on the back of the man's sunburned neck. I couldn't tell if the look he gave me contained hatred, but it could have said a million things.

"I'm going to redo this zip-tie, okay?" I called to the guard.

"Uh, okay, Sergeant."

I half expected the Marine to stop me from cutting the band on the man's wrist, but with a gun in his face the prisoner remained very still, keeping his hands in the same place after my knife cut through the thick plastic.

"Rub your wrist."

I walked in front of the prisoner and mimed massaging my wrist. The man imitated me, stiffly rubbing the raw purple and red marks on his wrists. After a few seconds the color returned to his hands and he winced, sharply sucking air through his teeth.

"Alright, I'm going to tie you back up."

The man slowly eased his hands behind his back and I fastened them with another set of plastic cuffs, slightly looser than before.

"Dude, these guys aren't saying anything," Cat proclaimed.

I looked at him and nodded. Enemy or not, they could stand to benefit from a little human compassion. Perhaps a simple act of kindness would make an impression on them and benefit us in return, later. It was hard to imagine it mattered since the men were probably going to prison, but I moved on with the water bottle anyway to give the next detainee a drink.

An hour passed. We were beginning to think someone had alerted drivers down the road there was a checkpoint ahead when another sedan approached. The driver held a handkerchief out his window as a makeshift peace offering. We couldn't take any chances. The Marines flagged down the gray Toyota and its driver stopped in front of the wire barricade.

His identification checked out. The Marines waved him on, but the man wasn't content to drive away.

"Hey, PSYOPs!" The guard shouted from across the road. We'd retired to the shade of our truck and were reluctant to step back into the burning sun.

"We need your terp back here!"

The Marine directed our newest visitor into the holding area. Cat, Josh, and I walked with Sonny to the waiting vehicle. I wasn't certain if the man hid in his words the foundation for a future trap, but the story he told made our hearts race. It wasn't often Iraqis, especially Sunni Anbaris like the man before us, disempowered after the fall of Saddam's regime, willingly and actively contributed topical, actionable intelligence information. But it seemed this one did. Trojan horse or not, we nonetheless dutifully copied down the details he shared of where to find insurgent safehouses in Karabilah and plans for another attack on Camp Gannon.

"We want to talk to him again."

Cat urged Sonny to relay the request. "Get his phone number."

My team leader turned to me. "And HET needs to meet this guy, too."

The mood inside our truck on the drive back to camp was one of excited impatience. Cat could scarcely wait to pass his discovery on to HET and Major Knight, the operations chief. If they had doubted before, the information he carried would certainly boost our standing with the battalion staff, if it proved to be true. It could even help save Marines' lives.

9. CAT WALKS BY HIMSELF

Our reception was not quite as welcoming as expected following our return to base. Josh and I had just settled back into the hooch after refueling the truck for another mission when Cat stormed through the door. His angry steps clattered like hoof beats across the plywood.

"Damn it! Damn it! I think I'm in trouble. Fuck!"

He sat down heavily on the edge of his bed.

"What happened," I wondered, looking up from unlacing my boots.

"Oh, I just told that asshole Hart to go fuck himself, and he called Gerry. I don't know. I'm supposed to go back to Al Asad for a while."

Cat huffed out a frustrated sigh and lay back on the bed, covering his forehead with one arm.

This unpleasant friction between Cat and the information operations sergeant had been festering since our arrival at Al Qa'im from the dam. Neither of them could ever agree on whom should be responsible for what, and refused to compromise. Cat's brash personality hadn't made the situation any easier to resolve. Apparently their distaste for each other had just come to a head in the office and Staff Sergeant Hart decided to use the trump card of his superior rank to get Cat in trouble with our boss. There was probably more to it than Cat would admit, but I had to agree I didn't like Hart either.

"What about the mission? When are you leaving?"

"You guys are going to have to stay here and take care of it. I should be back in about two weeks."

After that afternoon, we didn't see much of Cat. He left the next day on an early chopper flight, and as next ranking, I assumed his position as team leader. But with Cat gone, the team was just a pair: Josh and myself. Being short one man meant I would have to beg the Marines to fill the vacancy for us.

At the daily battle update meeting no one mentioned Cat being sent away, but I got the impression everyone already knew. People normally friendly to me avoided eye contact. Everyone else simply briefed their slides as if nothing had happened. I felt like an outsider, small and very alone. If the PSYOP mission at Al Qa'im were to continue I had to swallow any feelings of resentment I held and succeed in spite of whatever Hart or anyone else thought. Unfortunately, for the most part it didn't seem as if many of the leaders present cared if the battalion kept its TPT or not. Their priority was killing, not talking, and we were simply a rival service's novelty imposed upon them to be tolerated as necessary until some excuse could be found to send us away.

When the meeting ended I walked downstairs to the civil affairs office. Staff Sergeant Williams, the CA team chief, sat behind his laptop, busily typing some sort of report.

"Staff Sergeant," I asked politely, "could I ask a favor of you?"

"I guess that depends," he replied, still typing, "on what you want."

"I was wondering if you could spare one of your guys to gun for us on this mission to Shereya tomorrow. We're short one man now."

"Yeah . . ."

Williams looked up from his screen and glanced at Hart's empty desk and then back to me.

"I guess that's not a problem. Go talk to Z about it."

Z, another of the CA team members, was a stocky Marine sergeant of Mexican heritage known to his subordinates as a strict disciplinarian. Even so, I'd always found him approachable and friendly when he wasn't working. I walked back to the hooch to find him. He sat in a camp chair in front of the communal television, absentmindedly watching a bad copy of a pirated movie and cleaning his rifle.

"Yeah, man, I'll gun for you myself. I'm tired of sitting around here anyways. Where are we going?"

"Nothing major. It's some village called Shereya, near Ubaydi. Kilo Company is going to search some houses and we'll probably just do a civilian noninterference message and pass out some lickey-cheweys."

"Yeah, I'm down. Too easy. Just let me know."

Before dawn our vehicles assembled in front of the battalion headquarters. Marines scurried about in the darkness, the lights of their red flashlights bobbing like lightning bugs, conducting radio checks and a final convoy brief around the sand table. Z sat in the turret's swing seat, tapping his feet on the radio mount. It was dark, but would soon be too light for night vision goggles. Josh carefully followed the dim black-out lights of the vehicle in front of us out the gate. As the miles passed the sky grew lighter, and where before only two dim points of light were visible we could make out the shapes of vehicles.

The desert always seemed most peaceful in the morning when the heat had not yet reached its peak. Occasionally one could spot a rabbit or kangaroo rat hopping toward a shady spot to rest the day away after a night of foraging. A few wispy pink clouds lay dying in the distance. I slouched in the cramped troop commander's seat and leaned my helmet against the thick pane of bulletproof glass, reflecting quietly on the passing landscape and underappreciated beauty of the Iraqi dawn.

"Flash! Flash! All victors, convoy commander! We have a FRAGO from battalion!"

I'd turned the speaker up loud, paranoid that I might miss anything during the previous period of radio silence. The startlingly loud announcement burst the static bubble of white noise. I reached up to turn down the speaker and held the handset close to my ear.

A FRAGO meant we'd received a high-priority fragmentary order from headquarters. Captain Lund's familiar voice continued through the handset.

"Listen up, gentlemen; we're going to deviate from our current course. Battalion just sent us the grid location to what is likely Zarqawi's safe house. We have good intelligence that says he is in the house right now. Break. Task force is en route to the objective, so let's not waste any time. This is our chance to get this asshole."

The lead vehicle made a sharp left turn and increased speed.

Abu Musab al-Zarqawi was the Jordanian-born leader of Al-Qaeda in Iraq. Under his leadership the organization claimed responsibility for hundreds of bombings and assassinations, leading the U.S. government to offer a $25 million reward for information leading to his capture. He had gained personal notoriety for videotaping himself cutting off the heads of his American prisoners. His capture or death could potentially inflict a significant blow to the insurgency and would mean a major propaganda victory for Coalition Forces, at least until the next figurehead of evil replaced him.

Our objective appeared in the distance, a nondescript adobe structure nearly camouflaged by the surrounding sand, alone in the midst of nothingness. It had probably been a shepherd's shelter once. A rusty orange and white taxi sat next to the building. Clouds of dust rose in the opposite direction, signaling the approach of another convoy of Humvees, and together we surrounded the objective. There could be no escape from the ring of firepower trained on the building's doors and windows.

Two Humvees skidded to a halt close to the house and its occupants piled out to form a hasty stack at the front door. The Marine at the back of the stack ran forward with a shotgun, blasted the lock, and kicked the door in. In the same instant another man threw in a concussion grenade.

Boom!

Light flashed through the windows and the stack disappeared into the house.

"He's not here. The house is empty," came the report from the clearing team. "The lights are still on . . . we've got computers . . . bloody bandages . . . a shotgun.

Looks like we just missed them."

Zarqawi was alleged to have been wounded during an earlier encounter with U.S. forces, so the bandages seemed to corroborate the fact he had again somehow managed a narrow escape. Further inspection of the surrounding area uncovered fresh vehicle tracks leading back to the road. It wasn't clear how, but it seemed obvious the man had been tipped off to the raid minutes before we arrived. Maybe he had seen the dust, or perhaps he had spies posted along the way.

But the raid was not a total failure. In his haste, Zarqawi and his aides left behind valuable evidence of their past and future plans, which intelligence experts could extract from the hard drives of their abandoned computers. He also left a sample of his blood, which might yield a DNA fingerprint to identify the corpse we hoped to turn him into.

The Marines loaded all they could carry into their vehicles and we returned to Al Qa'im to deliver our consolation prizes to the intelligence shop. Zarqawi remained free to kill again, though with a few less secrets.

Is he too symbolic of terror for us to ever be allowed to catch him?

10. CLOSE CALLS AND CHICKEN WINGS

Camp Gannon owed its name to Captain Richard Gannon, the late commander of Lima Company, 3rd Battalion, 7th Marines. He'd been killed a year earlier attempting to rescue a wounded Marine during a firefight. For his sacrifice he earned a posthumous promotion and a Silver Star, as well as the distinction of becoming namesake of the tiny complex of abandoned buildings sandwiched between the Syrian border and the restive town of Husaybah. The camp he defended continued to suffer a near-daily onslaught of sniper and mortar fire from the apartment buildings and alleyways just a few yards outside its HESCO walls.

Only weeks before, the Marines of India Company, the camp's current occupants, had defeated a coordinated attack by up to a hundred insurgents who attempted to breach the perimeter of the camp with multiple suicide car bombs and overrun its defenses. Three Marines had been wounded and nineteen insurgents killed. The attack failed, but it proved the enemy still had the ability to plan sophisticated operations and amass sizable forces right under the Marines' noses. Armed with new information from an informant that they planned another attack, it was imperative we let the enemy know their hand had been tipped and they would not catch the Marines off guard if they tried again. The day after the Zarqawi raid, following the battle update brief, Major Knight informed me our TPT had been ordered to Camp Gannon.

137

We still had no word on when Cat might return; in fact I'd not heard from him since his departure for Al Asad. Judging from the office gossip I overheard on my end, the Marines were in no rush to bring him back.

One of the civil affairs Marines related to me a comment made by Staff Sergeant Hart that morning while we'd been out supporting a minor medical program in a nearby village, passing out activity booklets to children and talking to adults about the importance of proper sanitation while the medics bandaged the villagers' cuts and bruises.

The IO chief confiscated the case of Gatorade that Cat had stored under his desk and brought it back to the hooch to distribute among the rest of the Marines, saying, "I get at least one. I'm the one who got that guy kicked out of here."

At least in Husaybah I wouldn't have to listen to his vindictive gloating anymore. I submitted our names to the convoy commander of a supply run to Camp Gannon and we left the next day.

If Al Qa'im felt small, Camp Gannon was its runt sibling. From a distance the camp looked like a prison, with concrete guard towers poking up at intervals along a low gray wall of earth-filled barriers. There is a saying, though, that good things come in small packages, and the tiny outpost occupied an important point along a historical smuggling route between Syria and Iraq. Husaybah had in fact been an active international border crossing and customs station before the Marines shut it down. As our convoy of tanker trucks and Humvees bumped along parallel to the broken, rusted coils of barbed wire that delineated where Syrian territory ended and Iraq's began I witnessed that in reality shutting the crossing had had little impact. The vast border stretched largely unguarded and was extremely porous. Fresh vehicle tracks crossed over through several of the gaps and disappeared into the desert.

The city outside hugged the camp surprisingly closely. Both the southern and eastern walls butted against carefully arranged blocks of apartment buildings and grid-like streets. To the north and west, though less densely packed, lay the outskirts of the Syrian town of Abu Kamal.

Our convoy passed a smoking heap of burnt trash behind the outer wall and turned through the gate. I could understand why no one came to greet us. Surrounded on all sides by potential sniper-perches, we must have looked like tempting fish in the Camp Gannon barrel. Josh managed to find a parking spot next to a sandbag-reinforced mortar pit and I looked for a flapping American flag to guide me to the command post.

The commander's office nestled inside one of the few cinder block buildings in the center of the camp, its entryway protected by a long corridor of HESCO barriers. I pulled open the metal door and squeezed inside.

A gunnery sergeant with a coffee cup in his hand stood just within the low-ceilinged entryway. Seeing my unfamiliar face, he asked, "Can I help you?"

"Yes, Gunny, I'm looking for the commander. I'm the team leader of the PSYOP team from Al Qa'im."

"Oh, right. I'll tell him you're here."

The Marine poked his head through the doorway of a small office in the corner. "Sir," he announced, "the PSYOP guy is here to see you."

A slightly built but tough-looking man with a bony face, Captain Delorian, commander of India Company, emerged into the hallway. "Sergeant," he welcomed with an outstretched hand, "we've been waiting for you."

His handshake was very firm.

"Yes, sir," I replied. "I just wanted to let you know we were here and see if there was a time you wanted to sit down and discuss what kind of a message you are trying to send these people."

"Excellent. And I've got some ideas, but, uh, well, I've really got to finish something else first. It would be great if you could come back here around 1700 and we can dialogue the message piece. That should give your guys some time to get settled in. Gunny here can show you where to stay if he hasn't already. Sound good?"

"That works, sir."

"Welcome aboard!" The captain turned back to his work but hesitated. "One more thing. We try to stay inside during daylight hours here. If you absolutely have to go outside, you wear your Kevlar and your vest. We do have snipers here."

"Yes, sir."

I'd expected as much. The rumor mill at Al Qa'im painted Camp Gannon as the most dangerous camp in all of AO Denver, and I could practically look through the nearby apartments' windows over the top of the camp walls.

The gunnery sergeant led me outside to show me where we would sleep. He pointed to a rectangular structure made of HESCO barriers next to the speaker truck.

"Is that your truck there?"

I nodded.

"Okay, you go through those HESCOs and take the first door on your left. That's our transient billets. There's cots set up in there. Latrines are on the other side, nothing fancy, you'll see 'em. Chow is served over there." He pointed to a corrugated metal awning. "We are supposed to be getting a chow hall built pretty soon. We ain't got no lunch chow, neither, just dinner. And like the commander said, if you ain't doin' nothin', it's best to just stay inside. You folks need anything, just ask me, I'll be here."

"Okay. Thanks, Gunny."

I shook the man's hand and walked back to the truck, eyeing the dark windows of the buildings on the other side of the wall. Josh and Z still waited inside, with bored looks on their faces. I pulled open the door of the truck and called inside.

"Hey, we're staying in there, first door on the left. They don't serve lunch here, so, I guess just grab a couple of those MREs when you are getting your bags."

Our bedroom was a cave-like, windowless plywood box with a door at each end, buried beneath protective layers of sand-filled HESCOs. A line of fluorescent lights lit the space with a flickering glow that made one feel slightly nauseous. Along the walls several battered cots gathered dust. Long wooden benches and wooden pillars supporting the roof alternated along the centerline between the doors.

Z dropped his rucksack with a *thud* and dusted off one of the cots.

"So, what's on the agenda?"

"Nothing until 1700. I've got some meeting with the commander. We're just hanging out until then."

"You guys want to play spades?"

Josh looked up from spreading his sleeping bag on his cot.

"That depends. Do you want to get beat?"

"Oh, big words from a little man!" Z exclaimed. "Bring it! Me and my man Sonny are going to kick your ass!"

Captain Delorian explained the situation faced by his men in frank detail. His neighbors in Husaybah were so hostile that what few patrols he allowed to enter the city faced certain ambush. Daily mortar and sniper fire forced his Marines to take cover during daylight hours. Attacks on resupply convoys meant they often went without water for showers or fresh food. With only one company of Marines at his disposal, he could ill-afford to launch reprisals or sustain casualties, and so they waited inside the protection of the base as a matter of survival.

Outside, the insurgents boldly trafficked an endless stream of weapons and fighters from Syria, Sudan, Chechnya, and Saudi Arabia. Zarqawi himself allegedly made speeches openly in the city.

Occasionally India Company directed airstrikes against the enemy's safehouses, but for the most part their operations were reactionary. Camp Gannon was an island, isolated from support and surrounded by sharks. It was a credit to the captain's men they had recently defeated an attempt to overrun the base involving multiple car bombs and several dozens of fighters. More significantly, however, the attack exposed the level of audacity the Marines faced in an enemy who was not simply trying to achieve martyrdom, but who sincerely believed they could win despite the Americans' technological advantages.

"We need to let these people know," he said gravely, "that we are not going anywhere. The people of this town are getting sick of the foreign fighters and terrorists. I've heard it myself from the sheiks. These terrorists can't be allowed to think they can attack us without repercussions. I want to send a message to the people that sooner or later they are going to have to work with us and that we haven't forgotten about them. Believe me, we've got big plans for Husaybah."

"I've written a script that might fit in with that theme, if you'd like to look at it, sir."

I passed a page of handwritten notes across the desk.

"Hmm." With a furrowed brow the captain studied my work. "This is a good start. I'd like to make a few changes, but I like where you are going with this. I can have it back to you tonight. Does that work for you? So, let's shoot for doing this tomorrow morning. Does that give you enough time to translate and record this?"

"Yes, sir. It should only take about thirty minutes to have everything ready. I'd recommend broadcasting around 1000, sir. We shouldn't try to compete with the morning prayer, and by that time everyone will be awake and probably going to the market to get lunch and such."

"Okay, I agree. Excellent. Let me work on this and I'll have someone find you when I'm done. Thank you, Sergeant."

"Thank you, sir. We'll be over in the transient billets."

After the meeting I walked back to the barracks, still unnerved by how abandoned the camp seemed. The only visible movement was that of the American flag brushing against its pole and a plastic bag blown on the wind. I walked inside and removed my helmet. Z and Sonny still slept on their cots. Josh lay on his back reading the same book on Buddhist philosophy he'd been obsessing over for weeks. He turned his head and laid the paperback on his chest.

"So?"

"So, we are going to broadcast around ten tomorrow. The commander is making some changes to the script, but he said he would get it back to us tonight. Should be plenty of time to get everything set up. I'm not exactly sure where he wants us to go yet, but I guess we'll work that out tomorrow morning."

I started to rip the Velcro closure of my body armor open, but hesitated. My stomach growled.

Time to find those latrines.

The inconvenience of having to wear armor to go to the bathroom wasn't anything I'd ever contemplated before. We only ever took the vests off when we felt safe. It was telling that the security situation at Camp Gannon was such we were discouraged from walking around inside the perimeter without them. Wearing armor was a tacit admission of fear, something I considered whenever we visited Iraqis in their homes. It elt hypocritical that we should attempt to convince them security was improving and they shouldn't be worried while we Americans swaddled ourselves head to toe in armor and protective gear. Our hosts must have sometimes regarded our argument as condescending. Since we didn't allow them to have armor or weapons, it seemed to imply their lives were not deserving of the same level of protection as our own.

The stalls were only about twenty meters away from the back door, shielded behind a sheet of plywood.

This should be lovely.

The smell of diesel fuel and sun-warmed human excrement grew stronger with every step closer.

Crack!

A rifle shot whizzed over my head from the direction of the block of apartments to the south.

Sniper! I ducked reflexively and ran back inside. The rhythmic drumming of a fifty cal returned fire from a guard tower. My heart beat rapidly and I sat down on the nearest cot with my head in my hands.

Maybe I didn't have to go so badly after all, if it meant meeting such an ignoble end.

When the commotion died down I cautiously tried again. When I reached the stalls, a powerful stench and a cloud of buzzing flies greeted me. On one side were urinals: white plastic PVC pipes buried waist high in the ground at an angle, with a piece of aluminum screening wrapped over the end to keep cigarette butts out. To the left were the toilets. The arrangement consisted of a plywood bench with a series of holes cut in the seat, through which waste dropped into metal drums. When the drums filled, the Marines pulled the sloppy mess from under the benches and stirred them while adding burning diesel fuel until nothing remained but caked ash and the lingering scent of burnt feces. I reluctantly submitted my bare bottom to the hot wind, stinging sand, and crawling flies to relieve myself. In such a place, so-called dignity was a selfish luxury soon abandoned.

"You folks are going to have to hold off on that broadcast."

The first sergeant sipped his coffee unhurriedly.

"CAG [civil affairs group] is out there fixing a water pipe, and we don't want to attract any undue attention."

He pointed to an area just outside the camp on a large map tacked to the wall. I scraped my fingertips across my sweaty brow as he explained the delay. The Marines had been conducting what they called "cratering operations," using explosives to blow holes in the roads approaching the camp to mitigate the threat from car bombs. One of the charges punctured a water main, and the civil affairs team had ventured into the city to asses the damage before the lack of water induced the townspeople to protest at the gate.

"We're in no rush, First Sergeant. How long is it going to take?"

"Oh, I'd say they'll be out until this afternoon, at least. The commander mentioned something about making some more changes to that speech, anyways. Might as well take yourself a nap and come back tomorrow morning. There's nothing going on here."

"I don't think I could sleep anymore if I wanted to, First Sergeant. You mind if I stick around to use one of these computers? I need to try and get in touch with my unit real quick."

The first sergeant glanced over at his empty desk and gestured to it, quickly raising his chin. "I've got one over there you can use."

"Thanks."

I hurriedly logged in and brought up my email. I wasn't certain how long the first sergeant really wanted to stand in the doorway drinking his coffee. Only a few messages waited. Gerry had sent one about the last situation report, and Major Knight's said we should be prepared to stay longer in Camp Gannon. It suited me fine. Conditions at the camp may have been rustic, but the operational tempo was slow. I felt slightly sinful for enjoying it; but, like Br'er Rabbit in his briar patch, I wouldn't have told anyone that I was. I tapped out an inquiry to the supply sergeant at Al Qa'im asking when the next convoy was due and sent Gerry a short report that we hadn't encountered any problems.

"Good to go, First Sergeant. Thanks."

I logged out and picked up my rifle and helmet from the corner.

"Any time, Sergeant. We'll be seeing you."

He opened the door for me and I walked back to my cot to wait. Josh and Z played dominoes on one of the benches, waiting for my return with their mission gear laid out on their cots.

"No mission today," I announced, setting my rifle down on my cot and shedding my armor shell.

"Oh, darn," Josh replied sarcastically, though happily.

"We should stay here. Camp Gannon is sweet. No missions, no one messes with us . . ."

"No, we are going out tomorrow, they just blew up a water pipe so they are trying to take care of that first."

Z grinned mischievously. "I guess that leaves time for you to get your butt kicked in dominoes, too!"

"We'll see," I scoffed.

The next morning I walked back to the command post to find Captain Delorian standing near the wall-mounted map with a pair of Marines in tan coveralls. He traced a route north of the city with his finger.

"Oh . . . Sergeant . . . " he greeted, "meet Sergeant Frank and Sergeant Martin. They'll be providing security with their Abrams."

I smiled and shook each man's hand.

"Tanks, huh? Nice to meet you. Is this where we're going?"

The map was an extraordinarily detailed aerial photograph of the camp and city, almost two meters square. A clear plastic overlay covered with grease pencil markings indicated protected zones around several mosques and schools.

Captain Delorian tapped an area northeast of the camp. "You can start out here, by the ING compound. That should give you good coverage of Market Street, and there are usually a lot of people walking around out there."

The Iraqi National Guard compound was where that organization had once operated until being forced out by insurgents. The Marines maintained a foothold within its walls, just outside Camp Gannon, using it as an observation post and rifle range. I nodded and followed the long, broad street with my finger, imagining the sound of Sonny's voice echoing off the walls.

"Yeah, this is a good spot, because these buildings will funnel the sound all the way down. Looks like they do get a lot of traffic here, too. And then we can come up here and hit some of these main intersections. But we aren't going to be able to range this whole southern area." I gestured vaguely along the bottom of the map.

The captain nodded. "Well, we can try and hit that tomorrow. I want you to get out to the 440, too. We've been having a lot of problems with this area."

The 440 was an area to the south so named for the number of structures it contained, the same block of apartments from which the sniper shot at me on my way to the toilet. Hopefully, the presence of the tanks next to us would discourage him from trying again when we broadcast there, if he still lived. Sergeant Frank turned to me.

"Whenever you're ready."

"We're ready now, if I can just get the frequency you're using. Where do you want to meet up?"

"Ten minutes, out front."

I imagined our truck as the meat in a tank sandwich. It was a solid, comforting sensation. We rolled out the gate wedged between the two massive Abrams tanks, confident our escort would protect us from anything. A huge crater still marked where the car bombs had detonated a few weeks prior, and we swung wide to avoid the pit. Rubble of damaged and destroyed buildings spread across a wide radius, an indication of how powerful the explosions had been. The buckled roof of one of the buildings leaned into the street. When we reached a line of concrete Jersey barricades marking the extent of Marine control of the city, the tanks stopped.

"Is this good?" The tank commander asked.

"How we looking up there, Z?"

"Looks good to me. There's probably two or three hundred people out there," our gunner called down through the turret.

I keyed the radio handset again.

"This is good. Be advised, broadcasting now."

I pushed a button on the minidisk player and Sonny's prerecorded message boomed through the speaker.

"Agh! That's fucking loud!" Z complained.

"Oh yeah, watch your ears."

The tinny recorded voice continued, reverberating off the windows of the shops which lined the streets. Some people paused and turned to listen, others purposely ignored the broadcast:

Good citizens of Husaybah, peace and blessings be upon you. The fight of the Coalition Forces is not against you, but against the terrorists. You have seen them in your streets and heard how they murder innocent people and children. Now they have murdered the governor of Al Anbar. On May 29, 2005, Multi-National Forces were being shot at from a building while conducting operations. Multi-National Forces entered the building and killed four foreign fighters and captured four more. Later, one of the captured foreign fighters informed Multi-National Forces that the provincial governor was inside the house. Multi-National Forces then went back in the house and found the provincial governor, Raja Nawaf Farhan Al Sharhi, had been killed by the terrorists. The governor was found blindfolded with massive wounds to the head. The captured foreign fighters admitted to doing this crime. Iraqi Security Forces and Multi-National Forces are continuing to investigate this brutal murder, for which the terrorists are responsible. The governor was a responsible leader attempting to prevent violence in Al Anbar and was helping to shape the future of Iraq. Foreign fighters and terrorists have nothing to offer you or your families and do not care about your future. They care nothing about you or the good city of Husaybah. They take over your homes and show disrespect. They do not care about you or your family. Even now, we have learned the terrorists are planning to attack the city of Husaybah and the Coalition camp without any concern for the danger they will put you in. Therefore, good people, for your own protection, keep all vehicles away from Coalition Forces and remain off rooftops of buildings. Coalition and Iraqi Security Forces will continue to fight those who threaten the city. Your government and Iraqi Security Forces are working hard for a better Iraq and a better future for you and your families. Become part of the solution for peace and prosperity. Help secure Husaybah and all of Al Anbar by reporting foreign fighters and terrorists to Iraqi Security Forces and Multi-National Forces or by calling anonymously to the tips line. Information is the power you have over the terrorists and criminals and will help ensure safety for you and your family.

The last dying syllable echoed back to the crowd, which stood as if entranced. More people had since come outside to join them, curiously trying to see where the sound came from. No one had addressed these people in such a manner since the last PSYOP team was killed the year before, not many miles away. They were either starved for information or actually interested, because the message seemed to have provoked widespread community discussion. They expressed a variety of emotions with their hands, ranging from confusion, anger, hopelessness, and frustration to agreement.

After a second broadcast I keyed the handset again.

"Broadcast complete. We're ready to move."

We left the people to their debate and moved past the rubble back to the gate. Just down the road a large blue sign read, "Welcome to Syria" in Arabic and English. Next to it stood the picture of a dead man.

A wooden knock on the door woke us from our afternoon nap. The door creaked open before we'd had a chance to answer and a young Marine poked his head inside.

"Excuse me, do you guys have a minute? We're trying to get as many hands as possible to help unload one of these refrigerators out here."

I rubbed my eyes and sat up on the cot.

"Yeah, I guess so. What's going on now?"

"One of the refrigerator containers they keep the food in went tits-up, so they are trying to cross-load the stuff that won't go bad into the broken one and move all the perishable stuff into the one that's still good. Just trying to get as many people working on it as possible to make it go faster."

"Yeah, sure thing. We'll be there."

"Thanks, Sergeant."

The Marine let go of the door and it slowly creaked shut. I kicked the end of Josh's cot.

"Wake up, dude, let's go help these Marines move their chicken wings."

On the other side of the HESCOs, two large shipping containers with fans on the back sat next to each other, one humming, the other silent. A chain of Marines wearing body armor over their T-shirts mechanically passed boxes of food down to a large pile being sorted by more Marines into smaller stacks of perishable and nonperishable food items. Another line passed the perishable boxes back up. Josh and I each filled a gap in the chain and started passing boxes.

The cardboard boxes were white and cold, simply marked with their contents: *Corn. Beef patties. Chicken nuggets.*

"They've been holding out on us," I remarked.

"Supposed to be barbeque chicken tonight," the Marine next to me declared, with notable enthusiasm.

"Nice!"

We made quick work of unloading the broken refrigerator, and the head of the line of Marines moved inside onto the freshly exposed floor of the container. The chain moved with a steady rhythm, ferrying the frozen meats over a centipede-like conveyor belt of sweaty forearms.

"I claim this!"

The Marine next to me diverted a case of Mountain Dew to the ground behind his feet and quickly turned back around to catch the next box.

I did the same with a case of Red Bull.

"I think I can find a home for these!"

Josh stood in line across from me. His eyes lit up at the sight of the coveted drinks behind my boots. He nodded emphatically, and with a broad grin on his face tapped his belly.

"You're an addict," I told him.

"You better believe," he admitted.

Half an hour later the broken refrigerator had been emptied of everything but soft drinks and dried food. My forearms burned from the buildup of lactic acid, and I massaged them as Josh and I watched the Marines stack the last of the frozen boxes into the still-functioning freezer.

"That's a good workout," I declared.

Josh picked up the case of Red Bull and turned to trudge back to our cave. "Yeah, it's time to crack open a cold one now!"

I chuckled and followed him inside to wait for dinner.

Everyone seemed happier than usual to stand in line for what must have been an uncommon treat in the isolated camp. Green plastic tubs of chicken sent up savory wisps of steam from folding tables, and when I filed through, the Marine on duty scooped out an enormous drumstick with his tongs and plopped it on my tray. I sat down on a curb and held the plate to my nose, inhaling deeply. My first bite proved it tasted just as flavorful and sweet as it smelled, and I dabbed at the barbeque sauce smeared on my lips, staring into the distance and chewing appreciatively.

Suddenly a *Pow!* and the *Pom-Pom-Pom-Pom* of a Mark 19 automatic grenade launcher shooting back at a sniper from the southern wall interrupted our dinner chatter.

"I think I'll move over here," I remarked half-jokingly to Josh, picking up my tray and moving to the other side of the concrete barriers closer to the serving line. He moved with me.

The rest of the Marines remained nonchalant, busily tearing at their chicken and sucking on sticky fingers. I found it ironic that at Camp Gannon, barbeque chicken, not gunfire, was the rarer commodity. But I thought I could understand why it seemed there wasn't more reaction to the shooting. If any of us were to die for anything, if anything were worth dying for, it might as well have been for the guarantee of such a long-over-due proper meal.

Sonny and I sat quietly in the growing darkness on the sidewalk behind the command post, listening to the evening's sermon echoing from the minaret of a mosque on the other side of the wall. Sonny looked deep in thought, almost sad.

"What is he saying?" I asked gently.

Sonny paused before answering, as if carefully considering the proper words.

"Nothing violent. He is talking about staying away from the bad people and protecting the city. It is a little bit vague."

He stopped to listen as the speech continued.

"Now he is talking about the proper procedure for entering the house of a Muslim."

Earlier we'd listened to a different mosque's message recorded on a video camera by the Marines at the Iraqi National Guard compound. In spite of what the Imam's stern tone and guttural pronunciation seemed to imply to those of us who didn't understand Arabic, Sonny stated that the theme of the sermon was *patience*.

We were outside the HET team's office, having just finished a meeting with them to see if any calls had been made to the tips line since our latest broadcasts. Surprisingly, the HET team chief informed me they had received their first tip less than ten minutes after the broadcasts ceased. Additionally, he stated, the tone of some of the mosque messages in the past few weeks had grown increasingly critical of Al-Qaeda, and while not specifically supportive of Coalition Forces, they seemed less confrontational than usual. Both indicators were but a few of many in a widening rift between the townspeople and the insurgents. The people of Husaybah grew gradually more confident in their public condemnation of terrorist atrocities and less fearful of reprisals. One of the tips even purported to give the location of Zarqawi's newest hiding place.

We made so many broadcasts into the city over the course of a few days that the auxiliary cable to the minidisk player burned out. I couldn't help but think the people interpreted our renewed interest in their town as a sign of solidarity, or maybe part of preparations for an impending assault on Husaybah. Perhaps the brutalities inflicted on them by the terrorists simply made us the lesser of two evils.

Whatever their understanding, it seemed they were at last willing to work with the Americans. Tips were up, attacks were down, and reports said that the sounds of gunfire we heard at night came not from fire directed at the base, but from battles between local tribal fighters and foreign insurgents.

Maybe our messages really did have an effect. Or maybe they are tired of being told what to do by a bunch of foreign religious fanatics. They just needed the incentive of thinking we would back them up if they chose to fight.

But we wouldn't stay to discover the true motivations behind Husaybah's new complicity. When I checked my email, a message from Major Knight summoned us back to begin preparations for the next major operation, one they called "Spear." A supply convoy was expected to arrive the next day, and we were to follow it to Al Qa'im.

The convoy arrived an hour late. I said my farewells to Captain Delorian and Camp Gannon and arranged to join the convoy after they dropped off their cargo of generator fuel and water.

Our staging and departure was thankfully uneventful, though nonetheless tensely expectant. The last convoy to leave had been mortared on the way out the gate.

All seemed routine on the road back until,

WHAM!

I felt like someone had tapped me on top of the head, and my ears rang with a high-pitched squeal. My heart beat frantically, afraid of what I might see in the back seat.

"Fuck! Is everyone okay? Did we just hit an IED?"

I spun in my seat to look over at the rest of the passengers to verify they weren't injured. Sonny's eyes were wide with surprise, and Z held his ears under his helmet with both hands. The convoy stopped.

"Are you okay?" I tapped Z on the knee to get his attention.

"Yeah, I'm fine. Just rang my bell a little. It wasn't us." He rubbed his fingers in his ears and pointed over his shoulder. "The truck behind us hit a mine."

The truck, one the Marines called a seven-ton, was a six-wheel-drive monster so named for its large cargo capacity. Only the one behind us had five wheels. It's sixth had been blown off completely and lay in shreds on the side of the road. The driver looked shocked but uninjured. The radio confirmed no one had been hurt.

"All victors, security halt," ordered the convoy commander. "No one gets out of the vehicles until EOD gets here. I don't want anyone blowing their goddamned foot off."

The explosive ordnance disposal team did finally arrive to clear what turned out to be a string of newly buried mines, but only after several dreadfully hot hours. They had plenty of work to do elsewhere, on other roads. When they'd given the "all clear," the front half of the convoy continued on its way and the rear half stayed to guard the disabled truck until a wrecker arrived. It wasn't until nearly midnight we rolled back through the main gate of Camp Al Qa'im and fell into bed.

While walking to the chow hall for lunch the next day, one of the EOD Marines who had helped to clear the mines ran to catch up to me.

"Hey, Sergeant!" he called. "You guys were fucking lucky yesterday!"

"Oh? How so?"

"You know that security halt? Your truck was parked on top of a mine."

I looked at him blankly, uncertain of what to say.

"Thanks . . . I'm not sure I wanted to know that."

11. PAPER BULLETS

Back in the office, my email revealed more news I wasn't sure I wanted to hear. Josh and I had been expecting another team member would eventually be assigned to fill the vacancy left by Cat's dismissal, but instead of keeping me in the team leader position as we both had hoped, the detachment headquarters wanted to send a replacement from a different team, a staff sergeant.

"Nothing against you, it's just how the manning worked out."

Gerry tried to make nice preemptively, anticipating my disappointment with the decision. He, Cat, and Stephenson, the man slotted to take over, were due to arrive at Al Qa'im sometime in the next week to conduct an inventory of all the equipment and do an official changeover.

I typed out a terse reply, stating I would rather meet them in Al Asad. As a pay agent for the small rewards program I needed to sign some documents at the finance office there, and Josh had a piece of registered mail waiting for him that would be sent back if he didn't claim it soon. Besides, I reasoned, with preparations for Operation Spear looming on the horizon, Josh and I might not have another opportunity to enjoy all the facilities the big base offered for a long time.

Major Knight was not keen to allow us to leave due to the upcoming operation, but after some carefully worded reassurances that we really would be back soon, he finally approved our request to fly back to Al Asad.

Early the next day Josh and I hitched a ride to the flight line and waited for the helicopters to arrive. The Super Stallions came in low, choking us for a moment with a cloud of lung-burning blown sand. We squinted through the debris cloud and jogged up the ramp, thankful to trade breathing hot, powdery dust for the somewhat more tolerable hot, oily fumes inside the chopper, and wiped the grit from our eyelashes. The aircraft shook vertically into the cloudless sky and we watched Al Qa'im shrink beneath us.

Gerry waited at the helipad when we landed, with a broad smile on his face.

"Long time no see, guys! How was the flight?"

I hoisted my bag into the back of the van.

"Uneventful. How you been?"

"Can't complain. You got here at a good time. All the other teams are here, for once."

"How come?"

"Just a coincidence, but it has been nice catching up. You should come see everyone before they take off."

"Yeah, definitely. Where are they?"

"Oh, PX, sleeping, chow. I think Rivas and Munoz might still be down at the cans making leaflet boxes, though."

I watched passing rows of olive trees through my window in the passenger seat, noting that the scenery had changed since our last visit. Areas once piled with rubble had been cleared, and there were even new buildings under construction.

"What's that supposed to be?" I asked, pointing to the skeleton framework of an unfamiliar building, not yet fully clad with aluminum siding.

"That's going to be the new MWR [Morale, Welfare, and Recreation facility]."

"It's huge!"

"That's what she said," Gerry snickered.

I shook my head in mock disgust.

"Whatever. Not to you."

The cans, too, had undergone some minor remodeling, and a new plywood deck connected each of them down the line. The door of the first was cracked open. I jumped up onto the new deck and poked my head through the door to see who might be inside. Rivas and Munoz were barely visible behind a forest of haphazardly stacked cardboard boxes.

"Yo, man!"

Munoz greeted me with a wide grin, looked up from the box he stuffed with dollar-bill-sized leaflets and asked, "You want to help us make leaflet boxes?"

He slapped the top of a completed box that would later be dropped over a town from a plane or helicopter, bursting open to explode into a paper cloud of propaganda, raining down like so many thousands of falling, rotating autumn leaves.

"Sure. What do you need me to do?"

"You know how to make these, right?"

"Hmm. Don't remember offhand, no."

"Here. You have a knife? Cut slits in the bottom, like this." He deftly sliced four cuts in the bottom edges of a box. "Then take your engineer tape and put it through like this."

Munoz routed two pieces of white fabric tape through the holes to fashion a makeshift harness and turned the box over.

"Leave your ends out. And then just put the leaflets in."

With his knife he sliced open another sealed box, this one containing freshly printed leaflets delivered from the main print facility in Qatar. He lifted out a brick-like wad of leaflets.

"How would you like to have that hit you in the head?"

He smacked the brick against his palm. The leaflets had been printed, stacked, and cut so quickly that when the wet ink dried, it glued the sheets of paper together in a wood-like mass. Munoz twisted and riffled the edge of the stack to break it apart, and threw the less-than-lethal single leaflets into the box.

"You know," I recalled as I helped him break the leaflet bricks apart, "they say the first confirmed kill in Afghanistan was some guy who got hit in the head with one of these leaflet boxes."

"I don't doubt it."

Munoz stirred the full box with his hand and fluffed the contents. "Okay, when it's full, you tie your ends together and hook up the static line like this."

He attached a yellow nylon line of the type normally used to deploy a paratrooper's parachute to the white cloth tape harness and taped shut the

lid of the box. With another piece of tape he fastened one of the leaflets to
the outside of the box as a label.

"And that's it! We only have to do, oh . . ." He turned and tried to
count the unfilled boxes left over in the stacks. "About twenty more."

"Where are these all going?" I asked.

"I don't know," he replied, shaking his bald head.

"Karabilah, Ubaydi, I don't remember. I just make the boxes. Lots and
lots of boxes."

When we'd finished I retired to our old room a few doors down, somehow no longer familiar. It seemed strange and sterile, devoid of the comfort
it had offered after our first return from the dam. Al Qa'im felt like home
now, and I missed the familiarity of my own bed after sleeping on cots in
Husaybah. Napping proved impossible. I could not deny it felt relaxing
and safe in Al Asad, but for me, it was too quiet and artificial. Some of the
Marines referred to the base as "Camp Cupcake" because it seemed luxurious compared to the other camps, but I no longer cared to spend my
days haggling over DVDs or lining up for a morsel of over-cooked American fast food.

Stephenson, it seemed, did not feel the same way. After our initial re-
introduction he spent most of his time asleep or watching movies. He was
friendly but quiet, and I got the impression he'd been assigned to lead the
team specifically because he was incapable of upsetting anyone. The first
time I'd met him in the States I had wondered for days why it felt like I'd
met him before, and then suddenly realized it was because his spectacled
face had reminded me of "Ralphie" from *A Christmas Story*.

I wasn't complaining. Our new team leader seemed pleasant enough,
and other than the hour spent filling leaflet boxes, I did nothing that could
be called "work." I even considered word that our return flight to Al Qa'im
had been cancelled due to dust storms as good news, since it translated as
an extra day of vacation. Unfortunately, the impending operation meant
we could not afford to wait very long for another flight, and so Josh,
Stephenson, Rivas, Munoz, and I all crammed into their Humvee for the
convoy back to Al Qa'im.

The camp was crawling with visitors, including a significant contingent
of Iraqi forces in new plywood huts by the power station. During the night
even more convoys arrived. The tarp covering the roof of our SEA hut was

soon ripped off again by the prop wash of ceaselessly arriving and departing helicopters, which sometimes sounded like they would land on top of us. The flimsy walls shook under their thrumming blades as the choppers descended low and slow to the nearby helipad, returning from the covert insertion of snipers and special teams ahead of the main assault force to guard the approaches to Karabilah against IED emplacers and insurgents who might attempt to ambush oncoming convoys.

Sunlight streaming through holes in the roof awoke me the next morning. I lay in bed and reluctantly blinked up at the sky which shone through the jumbled boards, wondering how I had managed to sleep in spite of the racket. It had been an un-refreshing sleep, an exhausted surrender to fatigue after hours of waiting tensely for the operation to start, only to have it postponed another 24 hours. On the way to breakfast I stopped abruptly at the edge of the hill overlooking the chow hall, shocked by the unexpected vastness of the lines of armor and uniformed Marines below. This was going to be even bigger than Matador.

12. TINY, BLOODY BODIES

A t two hours past midnight the first of our vehicles left the main gate of Al Qa'im en route to Karabilah. I was somewhere in the middle of one of the convoys, and from my perch in the turret could see neither head nor tail of an endless parade of tanks, AAVs, and Humvees. We alternated between a painfully slow creep over the rocky landscape and acceleration to a breakneck pace made more nerve-wracking by the blinding dust and darkness. Several times we hurtled dangerously closely over the lips of fissures and ravines that jumped unanticipated from the blackness, snapping at the tires of our vehicles. At one point, as the convoy slowed, I thought I saw the shadowy outline of a town through my night vision goggles, but when I blinked it disappeared, a figment of the dust or my mind's fatigue.

The gray herald of dawn brushed the horizon by the time we reached the outskirts of the city. Several large explosions had already broken the stillness of the morning. On the other side of town intermittent machine-gun fire rattled like pebbles in a clothes dryer. Two or three bombed build-ings burned furiously, sending up thick black curls of smoke that tried but failed to darken the lightening sky.

We stopped behind a low hill and I watched a group of Iraqi soldiers clamber out the back of their troop truck. This was to be one of our first joint missions with Iraqi troops. They looked unconcerned and inappro-priately jovial, perhaps a bit lost. Some of them wore helmets too small for their heads. U.S. Marines from another truck ran to the crest of the hill and lay prone with their rifles pointed into windows and alleys, occasionally looking back distastefully at the Iraqis, who still milled around behind their truck in small groups waiting to be told what to do. One of their officers yelled at them to get on line and they, too, ran to lie at the crest of the hill, alternately watching the town and staring at the ground disinterestedly.

The assault began with a withering volley of tank rounds directed at the perimeter buildings. Whether or not anyone had been inside the houses, I couldn't tell. None of the town's inhabitants made any sign. The Marines used the term "suppressive fire" to describe shooting at potential hiding places without any clear target. It was hoped that if the enemy waited behind walls, he would be killed before he had a chance to return fire, or would at least keep his head down and not harass our advance.

Slowly, we moved forward, crossing a stretch of open ground before funneling into the empty streets. Infantry bounded up behind the cover of the tanks. Each element of the assault force had been assigned separate groups of buildings to clear, and reports of the different sections' progress crackled over the radio.

A muffled *boom* echoed from several streets over. One of the vehicles had struck a mine but sustained no casualties. The hair on the back of my neck stood up with the sensation of being watched. I dreaded passing each cross street and dark window. I scanned anxiously, intently from my turret for any movement or human shape in the shadows. My thumbs hovered over the butterfly trigger of the fifty cal, my fists wrapped around it in a white-knuckle grip.

The expectation of imminent ambush grew stronger with every block we drove farther into the city. I didn't like that I couldn't see over the high courtyard walls that guarded each side of the street, but I didn't want to fully expose myself by standing on tiptoe to look over them, either. Still the enemy did not show himself. Yard by deserted yard, we pushed forward. Cobra helicopters circled like vultures over Karabilah's heart. Distant gunfire popped erratically in scattered pockets as the Marines advanced block by block, almost uncontested.

Suddenly a double *boom-boom!* sounded from a side street.

"RPG! RPG! Contact right! We just took an RPG hit! Hajji's here!"

The targeted vehicle commander's voice shrilled with urgency. "ACE report!"

"No injuries, they're somewhere to our two o'clock!"

The convoy commander gave us the order we'd been waiting for. "TPT, broadcast now!"

Stephenson clutched the handset close to his ear, not wanting to miss the command. He replied before the commander finished his sentence. "Roger, broadcasting now!"

I'd been traveling with the turret unlocked so I could turn the gun quickly on target if necessary. I spun the speaker in the direction of a tall building as Stephenson pressed "play" on the first track of the minidisk. Sonny's prerecorded voice spat tauntingly from the speaker, loud and slightly metallic:

Oh Irhabi dogs, why do you run from us? Do you not want martyrdom? Are you too afraid? This is your chance to fight like men, so stop hiding like women! Are you afraid that when we kill you, you will be sent to pay for your crimes in Jahannam? You have two choices: surrender and live, and we will treat you humanely, or let us kill you, and feel the fire of hell. You cannot win today. Throw away your weapons and surrender now, or die. It's your choice.

We knew they would never surrender and did not wait long for a reply. At first I thought the shots sounded like they came from behind me. Someone with a rifle that wasn't an M16 fired single shots, probably a Marine sniper laying down suppressive fire. I peered over the chicken plate, trying to see what he targeted.

Another bullet zinged over my head.

I was wrong!

There weren't any Marines in the direction from which the shots came. I ducked instinctively, swung the gun around and pressed my thumbs down on the trigger. My fifty cal added its own *chunk-chunk-chunk* to the uproar of fire directed at the second-story window of the tall building, chipping puffs of powdered brick from the masonry. Metal links and empty cartridges jingled against the armor of the Humvee's roof and rolled onto the ground. The sniper didn't shoot back again.

"We're oscar-mike [on the move]," the radio squawked.

Our string of vehicles moved on.

The Marines practiced a very organized process of clearing. On the large satellite imagery map briefed before the operation each section of the city had been divided into zones and every building in each zone had been assigned a number to aid in reporting. The main thoroughfares were designated as phase lines. Each element was expected to call in when they crossed them so that headquarters could track the progress of the assault. We halted at the first phase line, delineated by a broad street. A neighborhood of large, gray, flat-roofed houses loomed on the other side. Once clear of the narrow road we'd been driving on the tanks and AAVs fanned out into the middle of the wide avenue and aimed their guns menacingly at the uncleared structures beyond.

Two of the AAVs with us carried an apparatus known as a mine-clearing line charge. A rack on top of their vehicles supported a rocket, which when fired, towed a rope of C4 explosive through the air that then fell to the ground leaving a long, deadly white tail that could be detonated to annihilate any obstacle it crossed. Josh maneuvered to a spot behind a cinderblock wall between two tanks just low enough that the speaker and gun poked over it. Behind us Marines scrambled onto every rooftop they could reach.

My jaw ached with tension. It seemed the day would never end, but our reaching the phase line proved at least that time truly passed. I swung the speaker around and watched the neighborhood beyond the wall, expecting the worst to occur at any second.

Stephenson keyed his microphone.

"TPT in position to broadcast the evacuation message."

"Wait one, TPT."

On the house behind us, Marine rifles scratched impatiently at the edge of the rooftop retaining wall.

"Okay, TPT, you're good to go."

I slipped a little lower in the turret, watching the alleys in front of us through my binoculars.

Sonny's hugely amplified voice buzzed in my eardrums:

Attention, good people of Karabilah! Coalition and Iraqi forces are conducting military operations to clear this city of terrorists.

For your own safety, you must leave your homes and evacuate the city. If you stay here, you will be considered an enemy. Do not approach Coalition Forces. Stay off your rooftops. You must leave now if you want to live. For your own safety, evacuate now!

No one moved. The Iraqi defense minister had broadcast a speech on national radio a few days prior, stating Karabilah would be cleared by force and ordering its evacuation. Reports indicated most of the city's citizens had either fled to other cities or camped in the desert to wait out the siege. I was glad it seemed everyone was already gone but apprehensive that the early warning had given insurgents time to prepare ambush positions. I swallowed a growing lump in my throat, anticipating the unseen listeners' reaction to the next message. The line charge-armed AAVs adjusted their launchers. We waited to see if anyone emerged from their houses, and after ten eternal minutes Stephenson lifted his handset again.

"TPT ready with bombardment broadcast."

"Cleared to broadcast, TPT."

Stephenson pressed a button and the speaker boomed once more to life:

People of Karabilah! This area is about to undergo massive bombardment. Evacuate now if you value your life. If you stay here, you will die. This is your last chance to leave alive. Good citizens of Karabilah, evacuate now! If you stay, you will be considered hostile. This area is about to be bombed. This is your last chance to evacuate!

The echoes died into stillness, and still no one appeared, friendly or otherwise.

With a great roar of gray smoke the first rocket sizzled high in the air, trailing a long unraveling coil of white rope. It landed at an angle in the street, the far end draped over the wall of someone's yard. It lay there for a second, looking relatively harmless, then disappeared in a thunderous flash of light and smoke. The earth shook under the force of the deafening blast and bits of rock rained down from a preposterously large cloud of dust that climbed without slowing. A stray dog that had been walking carelessly behind the vehicle ran yipping away with his tail between his legs. When

I emerged from my cover inside the turret, it was to witness a vision of the end of the world emerging from the dust cloud.

Where once had been a house with a stately columned entryway, there were only bits of concrete. The building's roof lay collapsed where the front yard had been. The entire street lay in ruins, destroyed in an instant.

The tanks and AAVs to our flanks followed with a barrage into the surviving structures, the heavy cough of their machine guns complimented by smaller caliber rifle fire from the Marines on the rooftops behind us. No one shot back.

"Should I shoot?" I asked. "There's no one out there."

"Everyone else is," Stephenson sighed. "Go for it."

My first few rounds from the fifty cal clipped the top of the cinder block wall in front of us. The armor-piercing rounds sliced through as easily as if the bricks had been cast from Styrofoam. I sighted in on a building that looked like a likely sniper position and fired a short burst. The window popped and rounds danced around the empty frame. I stopped and watched the puffs of bullet impacts on the buildings before us. Everyone shot at targets someone else shot at, but I saw no muzzle flashes or AK-47 wielding fanatics at all.

Stephenson tapped my leg.

"You might want to get down. They're going to drop a JDAM [joint direct attack munition: a smart bomb] on one of those houses."

I crouched inside the Humvee. All I saw through the windshield was the cinderblock wall in front of us and the electric blue sky above it, but I heard the jet approach, loud and fast. The roar of its engines grew to a crescendo and then faded, followed immediately by the thunderclap of its guided bomb's detonation on the ground. I stood up and saw the top half of the building I'd been shooting at obliterated, reduced to a jagged-edged crater of shattered brick. Somehow I expected there should have been more damage.

To our left, one of the tanks inched forward and pressed against the cinderblock wall until it bowed and collapsed. The gunner had a clear shot at a large house with an exterior staircase, and fired the main gun. My ears rang. Again, the tank fired the main gun, opening a hole in the side of the house big enough to walk through. A squad of Marines hurriedly clambered over the broken cinderblocks and stacked against the house before disappearing inside.

Moments later they returned, leading a shocked-looking man and two equally distressed women who could have been his wife and mother. A little boy no older than ten years old followed behind, cradling his visibly broken and deformed arm.

My heart sank.

Surely they heard us telling them to evacuate.

The house stood only a hundred meters from our speaker.

Why didn't they escape? Are all these houses occupied?

The Marines led the family to the back of an AAV and the vehicle drove away.

It was late afternoon. The Marine leadership declared we'd advanced far enough, and ordered that the big house be fortified as an overnight stronghold. Josh, Stephenson, and I gathered our gear and walked toward the gaping hole in the wall, hoping to claim a comfortable sleeping spot inside. I was happily amused to see a scattering of baby chicks had somehow miraculously survived the blasts. I picked up one of the peeping balls of yellow fluff and smiled as it stood unsteadily in the palm of my hand, remembering the chickens I helped care for as a little boy. Gently, I set the chick down and followed Josh inside.

The rest of the family still lay dead in the house. A track of child-sized bloody handprints crawled along the base of the hallway wall, leading to the spot where three little girls' blasted bodies had been hastily and unceremoniously rolled into a bloody carpet. The littlest one's pale, lifeless arm flopped above her head. Their bright pastel dresses were splattered with sticky, drying blood. Bloody boot prints and drag marks marred the floor. A large piece of flesh ripped from one of the little girls' bellies lay caught in the doorframe of the bedroom where they had died, unobserved or unheeded, for it had been crushed in the door and stepped on. The floor was disgustingly tacky from drying blood with spatters reaching even to the ceiling.

"Are we really sleeping in here?" Josh whispered. "This is fucked up."

"No," I said, staring dully at the bodies. "Let's find someplace else."

We climbed the stairs and lay our sleeping bags on the second-floor landing of the outer stairway. I looked out over Karabilah, a city transformed into a wide plain of smoke and fire. Cobra helicopters still strafed and rocketed targets throughout the city. The rattle of their rockets and Gatling cannons continued as darkness fell. Glaring red stitches of tracer rounds and flares against the night sky evoked a sense the aircraft were engaged in a futuristic outer space battle.

If anything, this place is going back in time, not forward.

Someone tried to open the door, but Stephenson had been sitting in front of it and it bumped him in the back. He stood up and kicked his sleeping bag out of the way, pulling the door open. Captain Lund stood in the threshold. He looked as though he hadn't slept in days.

"Hey, sir," Stephenson greeted. "Do you need something?"

"Matter of fact, I do. I want to try something a little outside the box. You folks can do deception sounds, right? Tank sounds, gunfire sounds?"

"We can do that, sir."

Captain Lund continued.

"I want you to broadcast tank sounds and drive around a little behind this wall. We need to move those tanks, but maybe we can make Hajji think we're keeping some here."

"That's too easy, sir. We're on it."

We felt our way through the dark house back to the hole in the wall. A group of Marines sitting outside threw pebbles at the dozing baby chicks. I glared disapprovingly, but didn't stop to scold them. A feeling of power-lessness filled me, the despair of a lonely man unable to stem the tide of cruelty and death that lapped over an entire nation.

What could we do but carry out our orders and do that which was expected of us?

My soul ached, torn between feeling a sense of contractual obligation, a desire to fulfill my duties as a soldier and to commiserate with my broth-ers in uniform while mourning the seemingly pointless extinction of so much innocent life. Not only the little girls whose stiffening corpses now rotting like refuse in the backyard, or the baby chicks that had survived two tank rounds only to succumb to the sadistic whims of bored Marines, but the countless thousands of other human lives destroyed by war and remembered only as collateral damage.

My thoughts writhed in anguish within my skull, contesting each other; uncertain of my priorities, uncertain of the truth, uncertain of my motivations.

When had peace become an unpatriotic notion?

Prolonging the war seemed akin to setting fire to a neighbor's house and then attempting to extinguish the flames with more fire. I felt at once very weary, exhausted by the heavy knowledge of so much violence and needless death. But I remained quiet as I crawled into the turret, resigned to accept my own sinful role. It was enough to know I was not the first to feel such things, and I remembered how the poet Tennyson had most eloquently summarized a soldier's role:

> Theirs not to make reply,
> Theirs not to reason why,
> Theirs but to do and die,
> Into the Valley of Death.

The Marines had been relatively lucky not to have suffered any deaths since the outset of Operation Spear. Their apparent invincibility bolstered a sense of exemption from death's toll that was evident in the speed and enthusiasm with which they cleared house after house, block after block. It ended the next morning when a suicidal insurgent disguised as an Iraqi soldier descended the stairs of a house as the Marines entered and opened fire on them. One Marine was killed. His buddies reciprocated by gunning down his assassin, but not soon enough to prevent their friend's death. It was a painfully frank reminder of the brutal and often unforeseen danger each man still faced.

We broadcast a final evacuation warning prior to the resumption of clearing operations, and had been surprised to see about a hundred Iraqis of all ages emerge from their houses waving white flags. There would be no repeat of the scene from the little girls' house. Constant bombardment of the town throughout the night had been proof of the veracity of our message and the vital importance of evacuation. Rather than risk being shot fleeing through the shadows, the remaining holdouts huddled anxiously in the cover of their homes and waited for a sign they could escape safely. Our broadcast assured them they would find refuge behind our lines.

The scene that greeted them required a certain amount of courage to walk through, though the consequences of not doing so proved motivation enough. I watched from the turret as crying children, black-clad women, and old men tiptoed past dead fighters in the street and under the barrel of an Abrams tank. One of the dead was a black-skinned Sudanese man who lay facedown where he had fallen after a futile attempt to attack the tank with his AK-47.

The refugees were obliged to consent to a body search by ski-masked members of the Iraqi Security Forces before being escorted to a holding area. While it was better in their eyes to be searched by Iraqis than Americans, cultural taboo forbade the women to allow themselves to be touched by men other than their husbands. Some of the searchers, as well, did not appear to perform their job very thoroughly. One family, fearing imminent execution as the searchers directed them to face a wall, burst into a chorus of terrified wailing. When it seemed no more people would show themselves we retired to the command post.

Captain Lund was incensed at losing one of his Marines. "I want a tank round in every building!" he fumed.

A well-known cable news reporter standing next to him looked shocked.

"Isn't that overkill?" she asked in a tone of disbelief and barely veiled condescension.

The commander replied with a single bluntly uttered word. "No!"

His anger denied him the ability to desire excusing anyone else from escaping punishment at the hands of his Marines for their perceived complicity in contributing to the morning's casualty.

Josh parked the truck between the command post and a small hut. I walked in alone. It was a simple structure, hugged by a small, shady yard crowded with fruit trees and grape vines. Like every other house, it had been callously searched for contraband and the drawers of the bureau in the single bedroom had been rifled through and left open. Amid the clutter and discarded clothing were stacks of clothbound books written in both Arabic and French. A lifetime of mostly black-and-white photographs lay spread on a small coffee table. I reached for them, and the mote-filled shafts of sunlight that pierced the window spun lazily in response to the movement of my hand. People in the pictures smiled up from beneath a film of dust.

I casually flipped through photo albums full of scenes of a remarkably ordinary-looking family enjoying celebrations and vacations, the same faces growing older as I turned the pages. A woman I assumed to be the occupant of the house appeared in most of the pictures. She had been plump and happy sometime during the seventies, judging by the clothes, and liked picnics by a lake and driving into the desert with her husband. Confronted with her ordinary reality, I wasn't exactly sure what I had expected to find, but there were no pictures of gun-waving terrorists or burning flags, just normal people doing normal things. I felt a pang of shame that I shouldn't have despoiled the woman's personal property and put the book down and walked outside to the truck.

I crawled into the turret seat and leaned forward with my head against the roof pad, listening to the play-by-play of cache discoveries and cleared buildings.

"Looks like we've got an IED factory here," one of the Marines reported.

"We're going to reduce it. Controlled detonation in ten mikes. All pax, take cover."

The explosion was much closer than we thought it would be and, surprised at how loud it was, when I looked up I saw the sky dotted with falling chunks of the destroyed building.

"It's raining rocks!" I exclaimed in warning as the pieces pelted the ground around us.

There were other more gruesome discoveries, as well. A nearby school had been co-opted as a terrorist training facility. The blackboard, where once children learned their alphabet, still bore instructions in the deadly art of bomb-making. As evidenced by the discovery of passports from places like Saudi Arabia and Sudan, the facility's students were not simply nationalist Iraqis determined to expel an occupying army, but crusading jihadists willing to travel to their deaths to fight an enemy they saw as infidels. Instead of textbooks, they had the Koran. Instead of music lessons, they substituted DVDs documenting the decapitation of hostages. Black-painted windows hid the reprehensible from view, whereas before they had let in the sun on growing minds.

How could anyone be so presumptuous as to claim their God endorses this kind of slaughter? Do the bloodthirsty men who have fought religious wars since the Crusades, who call themselves Muslims and Christians, really believe that an all-powerful God would actually waste his time to favor one side over the other so that they might control a few square miles of sun-baked sand?

I didn't expect God to raise his voice to contradict me. I didn't need further evidence of the ungodliness of man more than the four poor souls the Marines freed from the compound; they had been chained inside and their bodies showed signs of having been tortured with electricity.

Truckloads of weapons confiscated from caches within the embattled city piled up on the steps of the command post. I inspected dozens of AK-47s of all shapes and variants, RPG launchers, and heavy machine guns. There were a few .50 caliber weapons with thick, menacing-looking barrels, and even antiaircraft cannon. Mud and rust encrusted many of the pieces. The Marines found them buried in gardens, hidden in hollow walls, and under false floors. It took very little imagination to see the disastrous future that awaited some young Americans if the enemy had been allowed to keep such weapons. There were Kevlar helmets and armor, too, that the insurgents had once stripped from the bodies of murdered policemen. One of the blue helmets was still marked with the word *Police* in yellow letters. Each of the relics guarded a grisly history of secrets, culminating at our doorstep.

I took advantage of the down time to shave the past few days of stubble from my face, stooping over a small sink in a side hallway. I'd been surprised at the predominance of Western-style fixtures in Karabilah's houses, with familiar plumbing and interiors that would have complimented any American household.

A gaunt and dirty face looked back from the mirror, unsmiling and weary. I splashed water on my beard and drew it off slowly with my hands. The trickle from the faucet dripped weakly, only what had been left in the pipes. In a corner of the mirror I glimpsed a dark-haired man pointing something at me, approaching hesitatingly.

"Excuse me," the man said.

He was only a photographer, with an expensive-looking camera draped around his neck.

"Do you mind if I take your picture?"

"No, I suppose not," I replied.

In truth I suddenly felt very self-conscious that he should capture me so unkempt and idle, and quickly finished shaving with my eyes locked on the mirror.

"What's your name? Can I use your name?" the man asked in a slight

European accent. "My name's Johann. I hope you don't mind. I'm with Reuters. Well, actually the *New York Times* right now. It's just that, it was a good shot, you shaving. You don't see that much."

I shrugged.

"Listen," he continued. "Do you think it would be possible to go talk to some of the people down the street? Would we be able to get an escort? Just a couple houses down, and right back. Not to inconvenience you. If not, that's okay."

"I don't see why not. Let me go talk to my boss."

I walked over to Stephenson, who still dozed in the other room. Johann trailed behind. Stephenson lifted his head at the sound of footsteps.

"Hey, this is Johann, from the *New York Times*. Do you think we can see if they'll let us do a little patrol down the street and see if there is anyone they can talk to?"

Johann had come to Iraq by way of Denmark, and worked with an attractive but sullen young brunette named Samantha. Like a garment she wore an obvious distaste for being constantly stared at by dozens of love-starved Marines along with a feminine distaste for the omnipresent heat and filth. A hint of condescension darkened her face, but beneath it I detected a touch of uncertainty. She was tough and ambitious, although not overtly eager to prove her professional superiority. Still, it seemed she wanted to, if only to herself.

Josh, Stephenson and I along with two Marines walked with them\ Marine down the street toward a house on which a white flag hung listlessly from the roof. A stray dog barked viciously from an empty lot, but kept his distance. I pushed open the metal gate of the front yard and rapped on the door of the house, calling loudly, "Salaamu Alaikum. Peace be upon you."

No answer.

Sonny knocked again, calling, "Is anyone home?"

A voice answered from inside. The man was probably surprised we did not kick his door down, and opened it slowly. A time-worn old man, he had a white moustache and wore a long dishdasha of the same shade.

Sonny reassured him we meant no harm.

"There are reporters here who want to talk to you."

"Let me talk to him first," I interrupted. "Why are you still here? Why didn't you leave? Don't you think it's dangerous to stay here?"

"I know. I heard the radio say I should go. I heard the announcements, but I am old. Where can I go? The desert? I've lived a long life, I am not afraid. I fought the Persians and I am still here. Besides, I have my family to look after. And what of my house? Who will protect my house if I leave it?"

Two young boys came from the dark interior of the house to watch, standing under their patriarch's arm.

"What about them?" I asked through Sonny. "Aren't you concerned for them?"

"We are safer together. My son . . ."

A tear formed in a wrinkled corner of the man's eye and sparkled down his cheek.

"I have my son's family here too. You shot him driving his tractor home. He was a good man, an innocent man."

He pointed up the street to the burnt-out remnant of a vehicle. The Marines had destroyed several vehicles with tank rounds during the push into the city, which they identified as potential suicide car bombs. It was pointless to wonder whose version of events was true. The son was dead, or at the very least his father was a good actor.

"I'm sorry to hear of your loss, but sometimes there are accidents in war. You fought against Iran, did you not? You know things like this happen. There are bad people here, people who want to kill us. We have to protect ourselves. It is our job to make Iraq safer, and sometimes that means making hard decisions. Maybe sometimes the wrong people do get caught in the middle. We try to be careful, believe me. The terrorists will stop at nothing, even killing children, but we Americans do our best to avoid unnecessary violence. We follow the Geneva Conventions. We want to help you. That doesn't bring your son back, I know, but we are only trying to do our job."

The man rebutted my statement, morosely shaking his head in disbelief that I could be so wrong.

"Iraq was safe before you came. My town was quiet before you bombed it. Now I cannot even go outside. We don't have water." He sighed. "If you can just let me go to the water valve down the street, I can maybe turn the water back on."

"I can't make that decision. Our commander wants everyone to stay home. It's better if you stay inside, safer. We can bring you water later."

I turned to Sonny. "Ask him if he has ever seen strangers here."

I looked back in the old man's eyes. "Has he seen foreign fighters here?"

Sonny paused. "He says, 'Just you.'"

I squeezed my eyes shut at the old man's audacity and pinched the bridge of my nose. It was a true statement, from his perspective, that I was a foreign fighter, but not the answer I looked for.

"There are dead Africans in the street up there. He never saw anyone like that?"

The man shook his head.

"He didn't know there was a torture dungeon just down the road, where they kept captured border guards? He never heard a scream? *They* didn't think it was safe here."

I carefully watched the man's reaction to the news there had been such crimes committed so close to his home. He showed no surprise.

"If you say so," the old man replied. "I don't know anything."

Samantha looked annoyed and interrupted Sonny. "I'm sorry. Can I interview them now? Are you finished?"

We waited at a respectful distance to avoid the impression we might influence the journalistic integrity of the interview, and waited for Samantha to finish. Johann took some pictures of us with the family's goats, which grazed patiently on short-cropped lawn grass. When the interview ended we returned to the command post to load a few cases of water and Gatorade in the back of our Humvee and delivered it to the old man's house.

He looked pleased and surprised we had kept our word. We unloaded the water and were greeted by a swarm of children who took it from us as we entered the yard. One of them carried a silver tray of warm bread, which he offered to us.

The old man's eyes welled with glassy tears.

"*Shukran.*" *Thank you.*

"No, thank you," I replied, tearing a corner from my bread. "You know, we all want this war to be over, too. I want to go home and see my family. But no one will let us go until there is peace in Iraq. The only way there is going to be peace is if we work together against the terrorists. War is hard on everyone. But America is not going to be bombed out of Iraq, just like you are not going to be bombed out of your house. I've lost friends here, too. I know it is not the same loss you are feeling for your son, but I know your pain. I am a human being, just like you. We all have the right to want what is best for our families and live according to our values. It is unfortunate that we are forced to fight some people who can't accept that, and I know innocent people have suffered. But there will be peace again one day, and Iraq will have the future it deserves. I wish peace upon you and health and comfort for you and your family. This water isn't much, but I hope it shows we are sincere about wanting to help."

Silent tears moistened the man's cheeks as he grasped my extended hand with both of his own.

"Thank you. I pray that you will get to see your family again soon. You are a kind man."

I knew the old man didn't believe everything I said, but at least he saw me not only as a soldier, but as a human being, like himself. We shared loss and a longing for an end to the violence. We both understood the tragedy of war, and yet held hope for the future. We were both surrounded by the basest manifestation of human evils, but refused to be defeated by despair. As Sonny translated, the man repeated one phrase again and again.

"Insha'Allah.

Insha'Allah."

If God wills it.

13. A HIGH PRICE FOR VENGEANCE

"A battalion run? Are you serious?"

I sat up in bed and eyed Stephenson skeptically. He'd just come back to our hut from the daily meeting, and dabbed a trickle of sweat that ran down his temple with the fabric of his hat.

"We have to. We wouldn't want to ruin our rapport with the Marines. Anyhow, I don't think we really have a choice."

A "motivational run," as the Marines called it, was how they intended to celebrate the Fourth of July. I lay back in bed and sighed in resignation to the fact there would be no escaping it. It was sure to be less than motivational in temperatures north of one hundred degrees, and they hadn't mentioned how long it would be. If the battalion runs I remembered from Fort Bragg were any indication, we could look forward to at least a few miles of knee-jarring shuffle-stomp, all the while singing cadence calls to keep the rhythm of our step.

I wonder if their cadences are very different from ours. They are probably going to sing army-bashing ones. And what about fireworks? Are the insurgents going to salute us with a nice volley of mortars while we are all running in formation?

On the morning of the Fourth, Josh, Stephenson, and I walked toward the parking lot in front of battalion headquarters dressed in our battle uniforms. In garrison we usually only wore pistols, but in the interest of uni-

formity and mutual suffering we carried our M4 rifles since the Marines
would run with their M16s. As more Marines arrived, each of the companies formed neat lines of men behind their guidons, red flags emblazoned
with the golden anchor, globe, and eagle of the Marine corps.

"I guess we fall in with Headquarters Company," Stephenson said.

The formation stood four ranks deep and stretched the entire length
of the parking lot. Centered and facing us stood the battalion's command
sergeant major, who as a man of short stature was barely visible above the
rows of helmeted heads.

"Bat-alyun! Ten-hyuh!" he screamed.

All of us stood to attention as one entity, with an audible *snap*. I chuckled to myself that he'd abbreviated the command in such a stereotypically
Marine fashion.

"Rye, fay!"

We pivoted ninety degrees to the right.

"Port, harms!"

I brought my rifle up from beside my right leg and held it in front of
my chest with both hands.

"For-ward, hmah! Dou-ble tiiime!"

On the final command we each stepped forward, jogging in short and
choppy steps to avoid stepping on the heels of the men in front.

The formation smelled as one might expect of a group of men with
no one to impress, ripening in the sun. Powdery sand stirred by our feet
clung to every sweaty patch of exposed skin. My rifle grew hot and slippery
in my hands. With each stride my armor bounced up and landed on my
shoulders. The chin strap of my helmet felt scratchy and grew looser as my
jaw moved, making the Kevlar pot pound the top of my head. We chanted:

One mile,
No sweat,
Two miles,
Better yet,
Three miles,
You can't take it,
Four miles,
You won't make it.

Our column snaked around the Cobra helicopters on their pads, down dirt trails, and back up the hill to the start point, where tables loaded with hot dogs and boxes of potato chips awaited. A few representatives of the battalion leadership stood behind smoking barbeque grills, sipping nonalcoholic beers.

Colonel Dooney ascended a raised wooden platform and addressed his troops, raising his voice above their exhausted panting. The air was heavy with the scent of dusty, sweaty bodies and grilled meat.

> You Marines are the reason the folks back home can celebrate this holiday today in honor of our nation's independence and enjoy freedoms unparalleled anywhere else on the face of the planet. Each one of you made a conscious choice to join the finest fighting force in the history of armed conflict. You have each left your own nation, your own families, so that another country might know freedom. Your commitment to your country and the sacrifices you make do not go unnoticed. The American people are proud of the job you are doing, and I am proud of you and humbled and honored to serve with you.

The colonel's patriotic words were said sincerely, and the personal sacrifices of his men could not be denied, but to my ear, the speech rang hollow.

President Eisenhower once warned of the unwarranted influence of an expanding military-industrial complex, that the citizenry of the United States should be alert and knowledgeable enough to prevent corporations from dictating foreign policy. I couldn't help but wonder at the paradox of me, a citizen of a country that won its independence from British occupation through violence, stood celebrating the occasion on the soil of a country that the British had created and we ourselves now occupied. How prophetic had been our former president to foresee that the nation's military would one day become guardians of a New Utopia of corporate-military collusion that enriched corporations like Halliburton, Blackwater, and General Dynamics more than it ensured domestic tranquility or foreign freedoms.

If only they knew.

I lamented the state of what I imagined to be my countrymen's lack of awareness that permitted their collective conscience to embrace a war that no longer even pretended to be fought under the initial pretext of uncovering weapons of mass destruction, or at least allowed them enough comfort to ignore it.

If only they could come here and see for themselves how many dead children a half-trillion dollar defense budget buys.

If they did come, they would have also seen that the money bought plenty of nonalcoholic beers and burnt hot dogs, and we pawns were happy for it, at least for an hour or two.

One more holiday away from home. One day closer to getting back.

14. UNICORN BANDITS

Our convoy was already several meters deep into the field of peculiar-looking stones before I realized we'd entered a cemetery. The lead vehicle followed a two-track trail between the grave markers, unadorned flat rocks pulled from the surrounding desert. The village at the end, known to the Marines as El Guapo, was the poorest I'd ever seen. It seemed an unlikely spot to warrant settlement. There was no visible source of water nor any sign of crops, only a few starved-looking goats. Perhaps the village's founding fathers had been on their way to someplace better and simply gave up halfway through their trek. In fact, *village* was too generous a term for the crumbling cluster of mud hovels, too insignificant to be plotted on a map. There were many graves. Apparently El Guapo had been dying for a very long time.

The children saw us park our trucks behind a cracked adobe wall and came running. Their faces were filthy, their manners crude. Unlike children of other villages, they showed no timidity. We had barely stepped out of the trucks before they swarmed us.

Sonny waved his arms as if shooing away pigeons.

"*Imshee!*" *Get back!* he glowered.

He stooped to pick up a stone, threatened throwing it, and the pack of children momentarily scattered a few steps back. Their circle constricted again as the children jostled for position and the kids in the back pushed the crowd forward. Most of them didn't have shoes. Those who did wore plastic sandals too small or big for their dusty, stub-nailed feet. Their dark hair was long and wild to match equally wild eyes and runny noses. For all the poverty I'd witnessed in Iraq, most poor Iraqis were stubbornly proud of what little they did have, and diligently kept their clothes and faces clean. These children were impoverished beyond the point of caring what they looked like.

The commotion of their pleading voices provided a suitable distraction while another group of Marines circled around to surreptitiously enter the village from the opposite direction. I glanced back to the bunch of sand-tan buildings, scanning the dark rectangles of their doors and windows. The flutter of curtains, though there was no wind, confirmed that the children's parents watched us.

Josh and I stepped up on the rear bumper of the truck to open the hatch. The children surged forward, and even some of the teenagers whom before had felt too grown-up to beg for handouts ran out from their houses. They knew we'd be distributing something for free; it didn't matter what.

The children squealed with delight at the first sight of our cargo of soccer balls, stuffed animals, and school supplies. I slapped at the greedy hands that tried to snatch items from between my legs.

"Sonny! Make them line up! Either they behave or no one gets anything!" I yelled, snatching back a stuffed elephant and pulling down the hatch.

"Little kids first."

Sonny took a little girl by her grubby hand and led her to the front of the crowd. She smiled and laughed gleefully as I handed her the elephant and ran squealing back to her house waving the toy for all to see. Her older sisters, dressed in colorful headscarves, excitedly met her at the door to admire the new toy. Looking back at their unseen mother for approval, they both ran to see if they might claim one of their own.

"*Wahid, wahid*," Sonny cried above the mob.

"Line up one by one, or none of you will get anything!"

The children ignored him, pressing forward with outstretched arms. Josh handed a plush unicorn to a little boy, who clutched it to his chest and pranced away wearing an ecstatic smile.

No sooner had the little boy escaped the crush of the crowd than a group of bigger boys tackled him to the ground and wrested the toy away from him. He lay in the dust crying, defeated.

Welcome to real life, kid. A cruel one it is, especially here.

Knowing from past experience that the bigger kids coveted soccer balls above all else, I hefted one and threw it as hard as I could over their heads.

Get that, you little bastards.

All the bigger kids ran to intercept the ball as it hit the ground and bounced away, like jackals chasing a rabbit. Only the youngest were left. I threw another ball to keep the bullies at bay and passed down a replacement toy to Sonny, who knelt to console the crying boy. His little face brightened and Sonny helped him to his feet. Tears forgotten, he too ran in the direction of the soccer balls.

Josh and I hurriedly distributed toys, pencils, and notebooks to the good children who remained before the bullies could return, and shut the hatch.

One of them slyly met us on the way to the village, obviously disappointed he'd come away empty-handed, with the sheepish look of a pet dog who knows he doesn't deserve a treat. Still, he was not discouraged.

"Mistah, give me watch!" The youth tugged at my arm.

I pushed his hand away. "No, I need this. It's mine."

"Mistah, give me Playstation!"

I stopped midstride and turned with a raised eyebrow, amazed at the brashness of his request, and a little surprised he even knew to ask. He'd just beat up one of his little friends for a two-dollar stuffed animal, and now he pled for a two-hundred-dollar game system as a reward for bad behavior.

"What! You think I'm Santa Claus? I don't have a damn Playstation. You're getting coal, kid."

"Mistah, give me gun!"

"You're crazy, kid. Where did you learn English?"

"English? From movies! What's your name, mistah?"

"Moustapha."

He squinted into my eyes, half-believing me. "Nooo . . . Moustapha? Really? You Muslim?"

"No, I'm Christian. What's your name?"

"*I'm* Moustapha."

"It's a good name."

"Are you *really* Moustapha?"

"Yep. Really."

He jabbered excitedly to his friends. I heard him repeat, "*Moustapha.*"

I couldn't fault the boy for his desperate, naively outlandish requests for things he knew he could never have. He was only trying to acquire something to sell, or to distract his mind from the bitter poverty of his surroundings. He wasn't to blame for his station in life, and I could hardly expect his parents to discipline him when many adults engaged in far worse activities than begging. Maybe they even depended on him for extra income. Survival by any means seemed his main priority, not winning my approval, and my perception of right or wrong could not be applied to his situation. An empty stomach could make anyone forget extravagant feelings like pride and dignity. It wasn't for me to judge him without knowing the circumstances that compelled his family to seek refuge in a forgotten stretch of desert, whether it was fear, persecution, or simply acceptance of the status quo.

Neither was I prepared to lend any substantive aid in the form of food or medicine.

What is worse, to beg, or to give starving people stuffed animals instead of food or jobs?

If it were truly our intention to help the Iraqi people, we should have brought bags of rice instead of soccer balls, but helping them was in itself part of a wider propaganda battle, to appear benevolent in the media and to win the hearts of the Iraqis in spite of our record of civilian deaths and the fact that the schools and hospitals we took such pride in rebuilding were ones we had previously destroyed ourselves.

The Marines who had been searching for weapons began walking back to the vehicles, empty-handed.

"Hey, are you done? We're done," one asked as he passed.

I nodded and put my hand on the boy's shoulder. "Go home, Mustapha."

Wish I could really help you. I thought silently, and walked to the truck without looking back.

15. QUICK STRIKE

Rumors of another large-scale mission escaped the lips of unfamiliar faces in the more-crowded-than-usual chow hall. The operation was to be called "Quick Strike." Though I didn't recognize their faces, our visitors were the same attachments from Al Asad who had augmented our force during Operations Matador and Spear. It was puzzling that outsiders were more aware of the upcoming mission than, as residents of the camp, we were. It was frustrating, as well, that we hadn't known sooner; we might have been able to prepare better mentally to leave the oasis of the camp after having only just returned. As it was, we barely had time to restock our supply of water and MREs, refuel, and park back at the staging area. Granted, ours was the only PSYOP team directly supporting the battalion, but for months the practice had been that the three of us were assigned to every mission that left the gate, even the ones where our presence was probably unnecessary except as an extra gun truck. We felt underappreciated and worn out .

After lunch Stephenson disappeared into the headquarters building, emerging with a drawn, dark expression to confirm that the battalion was preparing for a major assault on the city of Anah, along the Euphrates—but the mission was on hold. A sniper from 3rd Battalion, 25th Marines, inserted ahead of the main effort, was missing and all other operations were declared postponed until the man could be recovered. The Marines' only priority was getting him back. All resources were to be diverted to the personnel recovery mission. We and the still battle-ready convoy we'd returned to base with were put on a two-hour recall, effective immediately, and could expect to receive an order to join the search at any moment.

Details of the incident were as yet unclear and any officers who knew something kept the information to themselves. There were suspicions a spy, perhaps an interpreter working as a double agent, might have betrayed the snipers, as it seemed very unlikely a team trained to be virtually invisible should have been caught off-guard by uninformed insurgents who just happened to cross their path. I felt the familiar empty, uneasy feeling of wondering whether someone I knew had been killed as we sat silently in the truck waiting for the mission brief. There were only so many snipers back at the dam. We'd chatted with them before missions when we were assigned to 3/25 and stood watch with some of them overnight back in Ramana. They'd joked and treated us like old friends without a hint of distain that we weren't Marines. They weren't cookie-cutter Jarheads at all. They wore their hair longer, in contravention of the high-and-tight norm, and didn't brag about how efficiently they could kill the enemy. Still, one got the impression they were true professionals, though too humble to ever admit it.

Which of them was missing? What happened to the others?

Something had definitely gone horribly wrong during their mission, something they normally would have been too vigilant to ever allow to happen.

A runner finished talking to the commander of the vehicle in front of us and, seeing him walking toward us, Stephenson cracked the door open. The man rested his hand on top of the thick frame and leaned inside.

"We found them. Search is off."

There was no satisfaction in his words, only a sober statement of fact. He confirmed the gruesome news we had anticipated but hoped against, but did little to explain the mysterious circumstances leading up to what had most likely been an ambush. It wasn't just one man; somehow two teams of elite snipers, six heavily armed Marines, had been surprised and overrun. All the men were dead. Their lifeless bodies were recovered just outside Haditha, stripped of their armor and rifles. It could only be assumed the specialized long-range guns would soon be put into service against the rest of us.

Operation Quick Strike may have been planned in advance of the snipers' demise, but in the wake of such a shattering loss, the Marines perceived it as a revenge mission. I expected they would be particularly brutal in their search for the culprits who had killed their friends, and the unfortunate residents of Haditha would suffer for it. The Marines' job was made even more frustrating by the fact our ununiformed enemies were known to exploit the protections offered to civilians under the Geneva and Hague Conventions.

They hid among the population, if they were not already one and the same, and occasionally had been discovered disguised as women, or forcing children to hold their hands in an attempt to appear innocent by association. There was no guarantee of who might be friendly or hostile short of catching them with a weapon or chemically testing their hands for gunpowder residue. There could be no consideration made for the legitimacy of their cause either, because whether they saw themselves as fighting for Iraqi sovereignty or were simply terrorist monsters who enjoyed killing, they knew their choice of battlefield put the very people they claimed to represent at risk.

This ambiguity, coupled with the Marines' thirst for vengeance, guaranteed both guilty and innocent Iraqis would die. The Marines' only sure defense against the nebulous enemy they faced was to shoot first anything suspicious and, while brooding under a cloud of anger and resentment, it was unlikely they would hesitate to do so. The ever-watching eye of the embedded media could afford some protection to civilians when cameras were around, as neither side wished to be portrayed as blatantly inhumane, but the reporters were never permitted into the most dangerous areas and dared not leave the protection of the armed Americans, which helped ensure that they saw only what the military allowed them to see.

Everywhere else was enveloped in the fog of war, consumed in a frenzy of bloodletting and the destruction of property. No one would be the wiser if the dead were labeled insurgent or civilian. No one would say otherwise for fear of being branded as disloyal. Even the chain of command only knew what the trigger-pullers chose to report.

It was certainly more palatable to report only enemy dead. It wasn't acceptable to admit some Marines lived to kill, as they had been trained to do, and didn't care enough to be more discriminating with their fire, or worse, targeted civilians intentionally. It was easier to see people only as numbers, to interpret every unexpected move as a hostile act, as a death sentence the Marines dutifully carried out. Anyone running for cover was running away. If a man was on his roof, it meant he was about to shoot. Numbers proved to the public the military was making progress. In such an environment the value of Iraqi life plummeted, especially following any loss of American life.

On those rare occasions when the military admitted to having caused a wrongful death, the gratuity paid by the U.S. government to the surviving family of an Iraqi adult male was only about $1,200, while the amount paid to the families of dead service members was $250,000, an amount raised later in 2005 to $400,000, with another $100,000 death gratuity. In neither instance could the money bring back the dead or ease their family's pain.

While our battalion prepared to join the fight, the battle reports coming back to camp confirmed 3/25 was already in the thick of it, facing an equally brutal and determined enemy. Already two suicide car bombs had exploded against Marine checkpoints in the city. Sickeningly, there'd also been a repeat of the AAV disaster the same battalion suffered during Operation Matador, one of the deadliest single attacks since the start of the war.

This time, the survivors wept over the remains of fourteen young Americans and an Iraqi interpreter they dragged from the unrecognizable wreckage of the bomb-blasted vehicle. Their deaths brought the toll of dead Marines to twenty men in less than a week. It was an especially heavy blow for Lima Company, which had already suffered so many losses. It seemed like further evidence someone armed the insurgents with prior knowledge of the Marines' plans, allowing them time to plant booby traps along likely avenues of approach. The Marines were incensed. Death would soon restock his inventory of souls at clearance prices.

After ten wearisome hours of driving through the treacherously uneven open desert under blackout, 3rd Battalion, 2nd Marines, finally arrived on the outskirts of Haqlaniyah, part of a converging assault force that included four battalions. We would rest until dawn and attack refreshed in the morning. But for most of us, sleep, interrupted by guard rotations and creeping anxiety, proved elusive. Between shifts on the gun I lay on the ground restlessly looking up at the clear and inky sky, counting the many normally unseen stars that decorated its velvet blackness. I wondered if I would live through the day to see them again.

At daybreak we pressed into the city. My entire body was completely soaked with sweat, not only because the rising sun beat down hotter with each passing minute, but because we knew the enemy had prepared a deadly reception. As usual, the streets were eerily devoid of even pedestrian traffic. The people were well aware they were better off avoiding us. In Karabilah we'd taken down fliers posted by insurgents that threatened the lives of the townspeople if they spoke to the Americans. The same fear of reprisals should they seem to favor one side over the other while its enemy was watching gripped the residents of Haqlaniyah.

We imagined every empty lard tin or broken bit of curb potentially hid a roadside bomb. The nervous tension ratcheted up with each passing block. Our tendons grew as taut as wires turned on a windlass. Every second that passed without an explosion felt like the odds grew greater of being caught in one. The mine-sweeping teams were very thorough in their investigation of each suspicious pile of dirt or bloated sheep carcass, and progress was slow.

We uncovered nothing significant but felt no comfort that we hadn't. The very absence of IEDs could have been a ploy to make us feel a false sense of security. The minute we showed complacency would be moment the enemy chose to strike.

Once past the ominously harmless approaches, we surrounded and seized a hilltop compound of three houses to use as a base of operations. The Marines rounded up the Iraqis inside and herded them into a single room in the smallest house. Sonny and Stephenson conducted a brief interrogation of the men.

There were six of them, four old and two young. The oldest, an impish, sharp-nosed, white-haired man in a long white robe claimed to be the site's caretaker. He said the compound had been home to a Ba'ath party official and his two sons, who had fled after the invasion.

"Maybe he is in France. His wife was French. I can't say for sure where he is," the old man said impassively.

The other men professed that they were squatters who operated an ice

factory on the property, except for the two youngest, who claimed they
were the oldest man's sons. I couldn't see any family resemblance, but as
detainees they were harmless enough. It was even possible they were telling
the truth.

The rightful occupants of the home had been favored by the previous
regime, and the house's owner publicly displayed his gratitude with a large
portrait of Saddam Hussein in the richly paneled living room. There were
several portraits of the previous owner himself proudly posing with clearly
prized Arabian horses, his sons, and with his pretty French wife. He wore
the same carefully trimmed moustache as his infamous leader.

By default our team held responsibility for guarding the six Iraqis as
the rest of the Marines left to set up radio antennae on the roofs of the
larger houses and to nap in their cool lobbies. We settled on a rotation to
watch the men and I went outside to inspect the property, leaving Josh and
Stephenson inside with the prisoners.

The estate was still impressive despite the obvious neglect that had
taken its toll over the past few years. Each of the sons' houses was a smaller
version of the main house, in the fashion of nesting dolls. The patriarch's
residence loomed above them both. An empty swimming pool dominated
the shared backyard. Next to it, a greenhouse with broken windows had
once shielded pots of flowers and vegetables, now dry and brown. The grass
had long since died and blown away, but I could see from the rusted grid
of irrigation pipes in the sand and dried clumps of roots and skeletons of
brush that the whole area within the compound's wall had once been
densely carpeted with greenery. Considering the decay, I wondered if the
old caretaker had meant to call himself a watchman instead.

Even our house, littlest of the three, stubbornly clung to its former
glory. Its grand wooden double doors were ornately carved with life-sized
horse heads reminiscent of the previous occupants' beloved Arabians. Passing through them, visitors walked across a floor paved in iridescent green
flagstones and entered a sunken, carpeted living room. One was immediately struck by the immensurable and unexpected beauty of a mural
depicting an ancient water wheel that flowed over the entire back wall.
Every room was furnished with American-style furniture. There were real
beds with coil mattresses, couches, tables, and Western fixtures, all of which
showcased the disparity between Iraq's rich and poor. There were bottles

of whiskey in the kitchen cabinets, too, which under the stricter interpretations of Islamic law should have been prohibited.

The bottles couldn't talk, but they shared much, perched on their shelf. They remembered a more permissive, secular Iraq, where private consumption of alcohol was overlooked though officially discouraged. Most of Iraq's bars and clubs were closed after the First Gulf War as Saddam attempted to curry favor with his country's religious leaders, the same reason he added *God is Great* between the stars of his national flag, but he still permitted alcohol to be sold in shops. Following the invasion, however, religious extremists had imposed much stricter punishments, closing down or blowing up those shops. People who managed to obtain, or worse, consume alcohol risked being shot. The violence was symptomatic of Iraq's widening religious and sectarian obsession, a rift that tore Sunni and Shia marriages apart and divided previously mixed neighborhoods. Christians and other minorities suffered even worse treatment. It was indicative of the misfortune Iraq's previously modern society faced; it was now plagued by a festering subculture of vengeance, mistrust, religious fanaticism, self-righteousness, and superviolence, made more disgusting by the hypocrisy of its enforcers, an insurgency that often found courage in amphetamines, opiates, and alcohol.

It was impossible to tell how long the bottles had been hidden, but it made me wonder if there weren't more secrets in the house. I shut the cabinet and returned to the small room where my teammates and the prisoners waited.

We sat silently for a long time, staring at each other and listening to rifle shots echoing in the valley. I didn't trust the younger men. Their presence was suspicious, and I believed the old man was protecting them by claiming them as his sons, even though they probably were not. The men shifted restlessly on their couch, tormented by their secrets. The old man cleared his throat and leaned over to address Sonny in a low voice.

"He wants to know if you would like some tea," Sonny relayed.

Josh and I followed the wizened old man to the kitchen, where he plucked a small tin teapot from under the sink and filled it with bottled water. He moved with the nonchalant grace of a man who had lived a full life, as if he were accustomed to making tea at gunpoint, almost as if we weren't in the room with him at all. He looked out wistfully over the desiccated garden and lit the gas burner without a word. I got the impression he would have remained the same resolutely obliging host even if he knew we had come to kill him. It was his tradition. The old man in the wisdom of all his years knew that civilization was only the agreement of individuals to treat each other with kindness. More so than the many governments that he'd seen rise and fall in his lifetime, he could depend on tea and his Muslim hospitality to remain constant.

"We should try to get some of that ice," I said, addressing the ceiling.

The power and water to our house had been shut off, and without air conditioning or a breeze, the room became a sweatbox prison. The last time I'd had a shower was before we left Al Qa'im, some days previous. I sat on the couch with my head back, trying to ignore the heat, sitting in a pool of my own moisture. I'd already changed into my only remaining clean T-shirt two days prior, and my uniform top was lined with squiggly trails of dried sweat salt. I was thankful to not be able to smell myself anymore. Not that anyone cared that I stank. We all did.

I couldn't smell the two clogged toilets in the house, either, or the other nine sweaty men in the room. I sat up and looked around at the scattered sleeping bodies of the prisoners. If they had families in town, their wives were probably frantic. But we hadn't been able to risk them revealing any information about our command center to the insurgency or to participate in it if they were inclined to, so they stayed.

I wasn't even upset that it seemed the command had forgotten about us in the little house, though I realized it was only because they didn't want us. The truck was parked out front where any of them could see it.

No matter.

I had already seen enough death in the past several months to weigh on my conscience the rest of my life, however long or short that might still be. I was in no rush to add any new scenes to my nightmares.

"Yeah," Josh replied, equally exhausted. "I'm down. I hope it's not all melted."

We shrugged back into our armor and trudged unhurriedly through an orchard of dead trees to the ice factory, a long nondescript hall clad in unpainted corrugated steel. A clatter of metallic banging echoed inside, growing louder as we approached. Two Marines had already beaten us to the ice. One of them knelt on the ground, smacking a metal rod against an aluminum box about four feet long, trying to break up the icy block frozen inside.

I hope they had some left for us.

The floor of the building was made up of closely fitted wooden planks covering a flooded pit. The boards weren't nailed down but instead were simply held up on each end by the lip of the building's cinderblock foundation. A gap of two or three boards had been opened in the floor, and in the space between them dozens of the same aluminum molds bobbed in a pool of cold water, all filled with ice.

Josh's eyes sparkled in triumph. He whispered under his breath in a singsong voice.

"Jackpot!"

The Marine with the rod seemed no closer to claiming his prize, though the longer it took the harder he banged and more frustrated he became.

"Goddamn it! Come out, you bitch!"

Every dent he made in the metal mold bit into the ice like a tooth, holding it in tighter. So far he'd only managed to extract a sad pile of melting splinters from the end of the tube. I looked at Josh, shaking my head incredulously.

"That can't be how they normally do it."

The rest of the molds were smooth and undented. I looked around the dimly lit factory, trying to deduce its usual operation. There was nothing that looked overly complicated. At the far end of the building thin copper pipes must have carried water or some kind of refrigerant. A beam on the ceiling supported an electric winch, which when the power worked, looked like it was intended to lift a whole row of the containers out of the water to another pool at the opposite end of the building.

"Ah! They must heat that water up, and it melts the ice enough to take it out of the molds."

I imagined the factory in operation, tracing the path of the containers further past the hot bath to a ramp at the end of the building, where the blocks could have been picked up by trucks.

"And that's where they dump the ice. We just need to let it melt for a little while. Let's take this outside."

Josh and I lifted one of the containers from the water and shoved it across the slick boards through an opening in the wall. As the desert sun blazed down, the ice block lost its frosty dullness and retreated ever so slightly from the walls of its prison. Josh laid a scrap of cloth on the ground and positioned the mouth of the mold over it. I tipped the end up carefully, so that the block slid out in one fluid motion. It glittered with a thousand points of light like a huge flawless diamond, unbroken. We each knelt at opposite ends of the block and scooped it up, carrying it on our forearms, using the muddy cloth to shield our skin from the cold. It was surprisingly heavy.

I glanced back to see the Marines inside had succeeded in gouging out about half of their block, and as more bits fell away they busily packed the shattered chunks into a plastic ice chest they'd brought with them. The mold was badly pockmarked and would never again work as it had been intended to, let alone hold water. The one wielding the rod paused, glimpsing the whole block we carried with a puzzled look on his face. As we walked toward the house, I could hear him still smashing furiously.

"God bless him, he's determined," I laughed to Josh.

But in spite of the Marine's persistence, Josh and I had still walked away with more ice and less time and effort invested. It seemed a fitting analogy for the inefficacy of violence.

By the time we reached the truck and finally set the block on the hood, my forearms burned from the strain. I massaged my arms while Josh went inside to brag about the ice. Stephenson and the prisoners appeared in the doorway, their bristly unshaven faces brightened by wide smiles. I posed with my arm across the icy slab.

How often could we expect to find such a rarity?

"Quick, take my picture!"

Josh obliged me, and we traded places. I watched through the viewfinder of his camera as he lifted the block above his head and brought it crashing to the ground. Glinting shards skittered across the pavement in dozens of directions. I gathered a double handful of ice and offered it to our prisoners. They took the pieces happily, rubbing them across their necks and faces, or simply enjoyed the coolness melting in their hands. We packed the rest in our ice chest in hopes it might chill our drinks at least a few more hours, and went back inside to wait.

In the morning a cargo Humvee pulled up in front of the house and a young Marine got out informing us the prisoners were being allowed to return home. It seemed fitting one of us should accompany them to the edge of town, as they'd been so hospitable through their ordeal it would have been rude not to say good-bye.

I clambered into the back of the Marine's Humvee and manned the SAW already fixed to a pintle behind the cab. I couldn't fully explain why, but for some reason, after all the time we'd spent together, I still didn't trust the men. Before getting in, I secretly double-checked that I had a round chambered in the pistol strapped to my chest, and for the duration of the ride I stood sideways behind the SAW so that I never had my back to them.

Regrettably I soon learned my suspicions were justified, and was thankful we'd never allowed them a single unsupervised second. After I returned to the house, we found an automatic pistol had been overlooked in one of the bedrooms, hidden in the back of a closet under a pile of women's shoes.

For all the pretended niceties, none of us could allow ourselves to forget there was a war still on.

Leaving Haqlaniyah was not without incident in itself. Even after all the weapons caches seized, car bombs destroyed, and the scores of militants killed, day after day, the Marines' fight remained a Sisyphean effort to push back an ocean's tide. We did not have the manpower to hold for more than a few days any gains made in the vast expanse of Iraq's largest province, with all its cities and villages. And, although they exhausted all of their military means to dam the waves of insurgency, after the Marines returned to their bases the enemy always flowed back into the cities again. They could operate anywhere they chose, while to stop them we had to be everywhere at once. Many of those we faced traveled to Iraq from as far away as Sudan and Chechnya with the express intent of catching an American bullet in their chest, so that their families would remember them as martyrs in what they viewed as a holy war, a continuation of the medieval Crusades. Theirs was a frustratingly foreign, difficult-to-counter mindset for us PSY-OPers, especially because against such a committed enemy our attempts to induce them to put down their weapons were rarely effective. The fear of death held no sway over men whose own lives meant nothing to themselves.

Under the best conditions our operations were limited by the amount of fuel, food, and ammunition we could carry with us, though sometimes it was possible to extend them with air drops or aerial resupply by helicopters. When outside our bases the supply infrastructure could not sustain operations longer than a few weeks at most, which did not allow enough time to ensure the total eradication of enemy forces or weapon stockpiles from the contested areas. If it ever seemed we'd wrested control of an area too easily, it usually meant the enemy had escaped to the next town, or posed as innocent farmers until we left. If they stayed, they fought to the death. Even as our convoys filtered out of town, the echo of scattered gunfire directed against other elements in various quarters of the city proved that some of them survived.

In my heart I knew it was preposterous to expect otherwise. While it was our prerogative as the occupation force to criminalize all aspects of resistance because Americans were dying, it was also disingenuous to claim the war's leadership did not understand the enemy's motivations. Certainly if the United States, a country which claims more than two hundred million privately owned firearms and many proudly nationalistic trigger pullers, were ever occupied by a nation that promised to provide a better form of government, that unfortunate army would soon be mired in a ferocious insurgency the likes of which overshadowed anything before seen in the history of unconventional warfare. I had to admit as well that I understood Iraq had become a lodestone for Islamic extremists who hated the United States for its support of the Jewish state of Israel, and therefore in their eyes also stood against Muslim Palestinians. They hated our audacious occupation of two different Muslim nations, and our direct and indirect contributions to the deaths of tens of thousands of civilians in Iraq and Afghanistan, which we arrogantly justified as a price those citizens had to pay for the more publicized deaths of fewer than three thousand Americans. To the jihadists it didn't matter if we did have the best intentions of protecting our country's national security at the outset of the Iraq invasion, or that afterwards no weapons of mass destruction were uncovered; it was only fair we stayed to help Iraq's government rebuild its shattered infrastructure and fight the hornet's nest of terrorists we attracted.

Their perception of us only as foreign, uninvited infidels was reason enough for them to detest our presence in the country. It could only be that we were blinded by our own self-promoting propaganda that we couldn't, or wouldn't, understand from their point of view why they so eagerly sacrificed themselves to fight against a hopelessly superior enemy and dismissed them as religious fanatics. For me, it was heartbreaking that both sides were so used to measuring each other in terms of religion, stereotypes, assumptions, and absolutes that we'd forgotten how to see each other as people.

Feelings of deep regret for humanity's habit of choosing up sides and then fighting each other to the death filled my wandering thoughts as I stood in the turret watching a Marine crouched in the gutter ahead. He poked gingerly with his knife at a pile of disturbed earth that concealed an IED. It was always misunderstanding, or unwillingness to understand each other, that brought people to the lows they reached in war. Our route to the river had been delayed while EOD cleared a snare of seven IEDs draped around the traffic circle.

Maybe part of the reason our enemy chose such weapons was because they could use them to kill us without looking at our faces.

It is emotionally easier to kill someone you can't see or have the possibility of knowing personally, the same type of thinking that makes it easier to gossip behind someone's back than to insult them outright. The same mind-set protected the psyche of bomber crews during World War II, so that they could sleep soundly after killing thousands. It was the philosophy that motivated the War Department to draw grotesque caricatures of Germans and Japanese on propaganda posters that redesignated human beings as targets. It is a policy of emotional distance and dehumanization. Soldiers can't be held accountable or feel remorse for killing someone they shared nothing in common with, who had never had a childhood, or a girlfriend, or a favorite movie. It was difficult to imagine what wars achieved beyond amplifying the very animosities that started them in the first place. Just like children bullied on a playground, losers nurse their grudges and in due course seek revenge, while the victor often takes advantage of the loser's weakness to extract unfair reparations or demand other concessions, such as territory, which the loser inevitably plots to take back. Additionally, war generally effects no great change in the status quo that would not have eventually occurred without violence. For example, slavery in America was becoming outmoded by innovations in agricultural technology before the

Civil War. Ultimately, the Soviet Union collapsed under its own communist inefficiency shortly following the Red Army's retreat from Afghanistan.

War is simply an evil accelerant, exchanging time for lives. If war solves anything, it offers only a temporary solution, and that one not very good. In fact, there are no winners in war. If our disagreements come to violence, we have all already lost.

The landscape that greeted us when we finally reached the river looked vaguely familiar, but then again, any of Anbar's streets could have been confused for belonging in another city. The uniformity was typical of Iraqi peasant culture. They were a traditionally pious, simple, and unassuming people. Houses were plain like the clothes their occupants wore, making no statement of individuality. Most buildings served only as protection against the elements, without unnecessary decoration.

I know I've seen that mosque before.

Mosques were the exception, an acceptable forum for extravagance because they were built to honor Allah, not express the pride of man. Our line of trucks snaked past nondescript garden walls and through a grove of neatly planted date palms, down a gently sloping dirt road, and emerged into a clearing by the water. There I saw the red pontoon bridge of my nightmares and realized I looked once more upon the site of our first battle in Barwanah, but from the opposite side of the river.

Perspective was not the only difference. There had been more fighting in the same spot since we left it months before, vicious by the looks of the rubble, the remains of heavy bombing. Only a concrete slab remained of the house our enemies once huddled behind between their potshots. Chunks of the former walls lay strewn across the yard in an unrecognizable jumble, completely scattered and leveled.

Despite the evidence of destruction the grove seemed so shady and peaceful it was strange to envision it as the site of such brutality. A closer look at the pockmarked, burned tree trunks and odd abandoned sandals and I could imagine what it must have looked like to face American tanks rolling down the street on the far side of the bridge, and rooftops crowned with rifles. I'm sure the trees still remembered panicked voices and screams, maybe of terror or defiance.

But we hadn't returned to Barwanah to reminisce.

I spun the turret forward so that our broadcast would funnel down

Barwanah's main street. Stephenson pressed a button on his control box and concentric rings of vibration appeared in the water bottle I kept strapped to the back of the speaker. It was an anticlimactic end to the operation, only an appeal to the residents that they should turn in caches and report terrorists to the tips line in exchange for cash rewards. It felt suspiciously as though the Marines were allowing us one small consolation prize, so that we could report our participation to headquarters despite having spent the majority of our time indoors with the prisoners. Maybe we hadn't made enough of an effort to include ourselves, but regrets in retrospect wouldn't change anything. Nonetheless, on the way back to the command post I felt disappointed and irrelevant.

Josh parked the truck under a date tree heavily laden with fruit. Instead of the usual dusty tan berries, the tree bore thick bunches of bright red dates.

"Look at those dates," I admired. "They're red!"

"Where?" Sonny wondered. "That's the best kind!"

"You want them?"

"No, don't worry about it. But the red ones are special."

"It's no problem, I'll get them."

I pulled myself onto the roof of the truck and swung a leg around the knobby tree trunk, climbing into the crown. The pointed ends of the fronds scratched my hands and face, but not very painfully so.

I, at least, am fortunate enough to feel pain. Pain is proof I still live.

I gripped the trunk tightly with my thighs and leaned back slightly, and with my one free hand pulled my knife from my belt and sawed through the fibrous stems to free several large strands of date berries. Sonny caught them as they fell, his lined face aglow with a look of childish enthusiasm. He rinsed and wrapped the dates in a plastic bag, then set them atop a stack of ammo cans beside his seat so carefully a bystander might have thought they were made of glass.

"*Shukran!*"

"*Afwan.*"

It felt good to do something only because it made someone else happy. Dropping the dates into Sonny's hands felt like dropping one tiny grain of sand onto the *good* side of the karmic balance of my life, an ever-so-slight compensation for all the wrongs I'd ever committed. I might never live

long enough to atone for everything that troubled me, but maybe I didn't
have to if I made a sincere effort to live a life that benefited others.

As much as I doubt it, maybe this life as a soldier is my destined role,.

It wasn't what I'd imagined as a child when I dreamed of being a vet-
erinarian or an archaeologist, but there were certain opportunities to help
people in the greatest need, a certain freedom in not having to think where
my feet would carry me, a greater zest for life when it might evaporate
without warning. My sworn obligation to "obey the orders of the officers
appointed over me," even though I didn't always agree with them, left me
free to relish the unbelievably rich sights and sensations of the world
through a body I felt privileged to still inhabit without the burden of personal choice or responsibility for the decisions that troubled me most.

When I was growing up my mother often told me I should "Relax,
and stop to smell the roses." I slid down the tree and dusted the splinters
from my palms. Lacking roses, it made sense that in the chaos of war I
should occasionally stop and gather dates.

*Sometimes life's most insignificant minutiae are what make it most
precious.*

We in the Western world call dogs "man's best friend," but Iraqi dogs have
no friends. To refer to someone as a dog is one of the worst insults imagi-
nable in Arab culture. Members of the canine species are regarded as scavengers and relegated to surviving off garbage. They are rarely kept as pets
and, in fact, are more likely to catch a swift kick than a gentle pat from
passersby. The back alleys of most Iraqi towns were home to packs of strays
that survived well enough to be called numerous, but they were notoriously
suspicious of humans as a result of generations of poor treatment. More
often than not, the ones we passed on patrols growled or ran away. It came
as a surprise, then, to see the apparent carefree joy of a pair of mongrel
pups who greeted us at the command post as we arrived to await orders to
return to Al Qa'im.

The puppies had obviously not lived a life of pampered privilege, but
they wagged their tails happily and whined plaintively to coax a few scraps
from the Marines' MREs. We sat on the ground beside our trucks and they
trotted back and forth plying the line like patrons at a buffet, sniffing
hungrily and licking their noses with the anticipation of winning a portion

of our dinners. Their muddled black-and-brown coats hugged their ribs tightly. With food so close, their hunger overcame their fear. They looked similar to African wild dogs and had the skittish dispositions of wild creatures to match, but eventually their noses drew them as if by magnetism to the snippets thrown their way, and they cautiously edged forward to wolf down bits of crackers and "Pork Chop, Chunked and Formed, in Jamaican Style Sauce with Noodles."

I tossed a small piece of beef jerky at the pair. They flinched and scampered back a few feet, seeing the motion of my arm that so often meant a rock hurtled toward them, but came back to greedily devour the treat. I threw another piece closer, hoping to draw them in. The dogs grew bolder and tamer as they came to realize I was a sure meal ticket who wouldn't try to hurt them, and before long they sat within arm's reach. If dogs can smile, I'm sure that was the silly look that stretched their faces. A string of saliva dripped from the corner of one's mouth, and he licked his muzzle in anticipation. I extended my hand and they ate from my palm.

"Take my picture," I whispered to Josh.

"What, so you can show it to some girl to try and get in her pants?" he retorted sarcastically. I rolled my eyes in mock exasperation.

"Dude . . . fuck you!" I laughed.

The Iraqis didn't mistreat dogs because they disapproved of pet ownership, and in fact most probably didn't actually mistreat them, only excluded them from entering their houses. Some families actually did keep cats or birds as pets. It was a long-standing cultural disdain for the dog, an animal regarded as unclean, that doomed them to life as outcasts. Dogs were considered pests instead of friends. There were no Humane Society shelters to keep them off the streets, and no possibility of going home with a loving human family. Dogs were simply ignored, worth no more attention than a rat. The only life they could expect following their birth was one of starvation, abuse, fighting, and disease. They would never be welcomed to warm a bed or called to play a game of fetch. Seeing the wretched situation of Iraqi dogs lent new meaning to "It's a dog's life."

I couldn't offer the pups enough food to fill their bellies. It was sad to think they would probably be dead in a few months, but at least they would have known kindness in their lifetime. When my bag of beef jerky was empty they wandered toward the rest of the Marines and inhaled the morsels thrown to them like little tail-wagging vacuum cleaners. It was comforting to see the men retained some gentleness in spite of all the horrors they'd witnessed and, admittedly, contributed to. Behind the armor and dust-darkened faces there was still a shadow of the cheerful boys they once had been, fighting homesickness and feeding the pair of strays that reminded them so much of their own family pets. For once we could return to Al Qa'im on a cheerful note, with fond images of contented puppies to distract our thoughts instead of mulling memories of the dullness of dead men's eyes.

16. "GOOD MORNING, HUSAYBAH"

Returning to camp did not mean our fight was over. Stephenson had barely finished sending his situation report before he was cornered by the S3 and informed that our TPT had again been requested at Camp Gannon. Josh and I got the news as we walked with our team leader to dinner. We had time enough to shower, clean our weapons, enjoy a few meals in the chow hall, do laundry, and write some emails home before pushing once more into the desert.

The route from Al Qa'im to the Syrian border usually wound overland to avoid the mined highways, but even off-road there was no guaranteed safe passage. The enemy had enough mines to spare, and a general idea of our routes, to still be effective, on occasion, at hitting the resupply convoys on their way to the Gannon outpost by emplacing numerous belts of mines along our likely routes. We had to be especially watchful passing through natural chokepoints and wadis as the insurgents knew what type of terrain our vehicles could not traverse and booby-trapped the areas where we were most likely to cross. It was also an almost hopeless exercise trying to detect the mines because the insurgents camouflaged them too well. Halfway through our trip the water tanker in front of us found one with a startling *bang!* that rocked the truck on its axles and shredded a tire.

"There goes our shower water," I remarked glumly.

It was an irreverent statement in the wake of what could have been a tragic accident, but in my mind, belittling the significance of the event helped me deny my fear the same might happen to us.

The explosion did no damage to the cab, but the truck's occupants were understandably shaken and their disabled truck had to be towed back to Al Qa'im. My teammates and I were too shocked at how preposterously often it seemed we narrowly avoided being hit ourselves to immediately feel any reaction. Denial was more tolerable. This strike made at least the third time a truck directly in front of or behind us had been hit. As the immediacy of potential death sank in, the familiar bitter tang of fear and despair again coated my tongue. The rest of our trip was darkened by the shadow of gloomy silence and dread anticipation.

How much longer could we avoid running over a mine ourselves? How could we not be worried, if even the open desert wasn't safe?

Statistically speaking, the chances of our luck running out seemed to rise with each near miss we avoided.

To our great relief we reached Camp Gannon without further incident. I felt the euphoria of a runner sliding into home plate with the umpire waving his arms and calling "Safe!". The camp was an ordered, predictable sanctuary after our nerve-wracking trek, even though I still remembered that snipers might be watching from the nearby rooftops.

At least there wouldn't be any mines.

I scanned over the HESCO perimeter walls skeptically as Josh steered toward our previous parking spot, keeping my head low in the turret.

To my surprise, I spotted a healthy-looking dog sauntering along behind a pair of Marines inside the camp! It was unmistakably their loyal pet. Normally all service members in Iraq were prohibited from keeping pets and mascots under General Order 1, the same order that forbade alcohol and pornography, but the Marines made no obvious attempt to hide their four-legged friend. The fact they walked openly with him through the camp meant their leadership endorsed keeping him, or at least turned a blind eye.

Camp Gannon may have lacked some of the conveniences of the larger bases, like regular showers, but its isolation permitted a more relaxed interpretation of normal garrison rules and regulations. India Company's Marines faced more pressing daily stresses. They could therefore be entitled some leniency in regards to enforcing all the military's bureaucratic prohibitions, especially if that prohibition was one that denied them the therapeutic companionship of man's best friend.

Regardless of their legality, the Marines' pets were service dogs in the same sense that dogs who visit nursing homes to comfort the sick provide a service. For the men who spent their days huddled in bunkers listening to the crash of mortar shells with no one to turn to but each other, the small comfort provided by a dog's gentle nuzzle must have been indispensable. The relationship between the dogs and their keepers was an island of kindness in an ocean of violence. There was such tenderness to be seen in watching the simple act of Marines feeding the dogs scraps carried from their new chow hall that I had to think back a very long time to remember anything more moving.

We spent three days with the Marines and their dogs inside the bunkers, rarely venturing outside except for food or the dubious relief of the latrine. Our days consisted mainly of playing cards and sleeping away the hours, waiting fretfully for the moment a runner would knock on our door.

Captain Delorian's days were occupied with far weightier responsibilities than talking with a couple of army sergeants. Husaybah had recently become the flashpoint of a new battleground, one between native Iraqis and foreign Al-Qaeda fighters. Several gun battles had erupted in the streets during the weeks prior as the locals grew bolder and more indignant in response to their treatment at the hands of militants. No longer would they suffer heavy-handed rapes and forceful evictions performed in the name of jihad. In their eyes, the Americans had at last become the lesser of two evils. Changing perceptions of the Iraqis toward the Marines had opened the door to negotiations with local tribal leaders to discuss the once unthinkable prospect of forming an alliance with them against Zarqawi and Al-Qaeda.

On our third day in the camp the commander invited us to attend a meeting of Marine leaders and civilian strategists. Josh, Stephenson, and I sat against the wall of a dark, low-ceilinged room in the command post. The seats around the table were reserved for the officers. I suspected one of the shadowy men dressed in a polo shirt and khakis represented the CIA, or maybe the State Department, though no mention of his employer was made.

The agenda was a discussion of the potential future of a new alliance.

At the time I had no way of knowing, but the meeting was to be one of the first toward the establishment of a movement called the "Awakening," a popular tribal uprising against Al-Qaeda that would mature to become the U.S.-funded, Iraqi-manned, private militia known as the "Sons of Iraq."

The man in the polo shirt cleared his throat. He exuded an air of gloating condescension, as if he were the smartest man in the world and had taken pity on us simpletons to share his invention of a secret weapon that would win the war.

"The great thing about these tribesmen is that they are basically cannon fodder," he said, with all the nonchalance of a man discussing what he had eaten for breakfast.

"All we have to do is arm them and they will fight for us. They are pissed off at Al-Qaeda already. We have potentially got the makings of a whole proxy army here. We need to continue to exploit this red-on-red violence! If it is Iraqis who are dying, nobody cares. The American people don't hear about dead Iraqis on the news. They will do our job for us, and your Marines don't go home in body bags. We couldn't have asked for a better opportunity!"

The frankness of the man's presumptions slightly turned my stomach.

Had I really heard correctly that our latest strategy was to use the Iraqis as expendable proxies, to press them into unwitting service toward achieving our own strategic goals?

We would send the Iraqis to their death with no more feeling than had they been cattle entering the slaughterhouse. They could expect no medals for heroism or death gratuities for their families, no words of thanks for their sacrifice or parades when they returned home. Yet they would shoulder the task without complaint, because the shame of doing nothing pained them more than the indignities they endured at the hands of the jihadists. It was their homeland they defended. They would think their fight against Al-Qaeda had been their idea all along.

I learned that the U.S. government had already been surreptitiously arming the tribes with shipments of ammunition and rifles, preparing them to fight the better-armed Al-Qaeda militants with the assurance they had the backing of the American military. But, they did not have our respect for their humanity nor our compassion. It was simply more cost effective and publicly acceptable to have them die instead of us.

Our team's role was to broadcast those assurances of support to the citizens of Husaybah in hopes of stirring them to action. This time Captain Delorian personally prepared the message text. Stephenson collected the finished product from his office shortly after our meeting. It was a single page, typed all in capital letters, which ran together like a Roman epitaph. Both reassuring and ambiguous, there was no question it was intended as a hint that the people should act soon to flush Al-Qaeda from their streets. Indirectly, it also questioned their honor and courage by implying that if they were not brave enough, Coalition Forces would do the job and rob them of the chance to exact revenge on the terrorists.

Josh and Sonny translated the broadcast onto a minidisk while Stephenson and I left the bunker to coordinate a security plan with the tank crews. Within the hour we were headed out the gate serenaded by a raucous squeak and clatter of tank treads.

Our invincible-looking guardians led us to a berm north of the city and turned their massive guns outward. Anyone who wanted to attack us would have to have a death wish. The tanks whirred menacingly. I aimed the speaker so that its sound waves would echo toward the crowded market street.

"All set!" I called down.

My bones hummed in sync with the intensity of Sonny's amplified voice:

Good people of Husaybah and Iraq, peace and blessings once again be upon you. Over the past few days many of the evil beasts who have been trying to bring hatred and evil into the streets of this good city have been killed or captured by Coalition Forces. But there are still terrorist dogs who care nothing about you or your families and who desire only to bring terror to this good city. Coalition Forces will continue to hunt down and kill those terrorist dogs. Once Iraqi security forces arrive they will continue the work to bring peace and prosperity to Husaybah, Al Qa'im, and all of Iraq. Brave people of Husaybah and Al Qa'im! The coalition forces respect the way you have stood up and defended your families honor by defeating the evil terrorists. They have killed innocent children, dishonored your holy places, and shown disrespect to your families and your homes. However it is no surprise that the terrorists have no respect because their own leader, Abu Musab Al Zarqawi is a foreigner who cares nothing about Iraq except to use the innocent blood of Iraqis for his own selfish purposes. Abu Musab Al Zarqawi, who is also known as Ahmed Fadhil Al Khalaylah, born in the city of Al Zarqa, Jordan, pledges his loyalty not to Iraqis, but to foreigners—which is why he does not care if your children are murdered and your honor destroyed. He is only concerned with his selfish desires, not yours, and because of this fact, the Coalition and Iraqi Forces will continue to hunt down and kill those who threaten to harm the innocent. Good people of Husaybah and Al Qa'im—your bravery and courage will bring a bright future for you and your families. Many brave citizens have been providing information that has helped destroy these evil terrorists. Join your brave countrymen and neighbors in their stand against the evil terrorists and call the tips line with any information. Coalition Forces along with Iraqi security forces will continue to fight against those who do not respect the people of this city and country.

By the end of the broadcast all the birds had flown away, and the countryside seemed oddly unfamiliar in the absence of sound. My eardrums throbbed furiously. At least for one more day, our job was done. We had planted a seed. It was up to the Iraqis to harvest the fruit, although when we Americans would entrust them in full deference to their sovereignty to do it alone I could not be sure.

17. OUT OF THE OVEN

Translated from Arabic Al Qa'im means something like "He who arises." In the Shia Islamic tradition the figure of Al Qa'im refers to an anticipated messianic savior who shall return before Judgment Day to fight the forces of evil. Though we Americans tended to use the name Al Qa'im in reference to a single town, the Iraqis understood it to encompass the entire District of Al Qa'im, including the region surrounding Al Qa'im, Karabilah, Ubaydi, Ramana, and Husaybah. And, though they were mostly Sunni, less than a week after we returned to the base we called Al Qa'im, the people of Husaybah arose to take up arms in fulfillment of their destiny.

Sound carries a long way in the desert, especially at night. On the fifth night of our return to camp the crackling of a fierce gun battle erupted from the direction of Husaybah. There were only a few shots at first, then a deluge of fire so great that the sound of individual shots muddled into each other. Bolstered by the confidence that they had American backing, presumably from further covert negotiations, the tribesmen had finally organized and made their long-awaited move against Zarqawi and the soldiers of his terrorist Islamic State of Iraq. The fighting raged for hours. At times the opposing sides met each other in large groups, assailing each other in a cacophony of violence, only to part again in a random popping of potshots. It was like listening to waves smashing against a cliff. First broke a loud crash, then the drip, drip of water off wet rocks. But I knew it was the salty blood of men that flowed and dripped, not the ocean's waves. What wasn't clear from so far away, once the sounds of battle ended, was who had won.

We had to wait until after the battle-update brief the next day to learn that the tribesmen's bid to take back their streets had ended in failure. They were farmers, not killers, armed more with desperate hope than a realistic chance of winning. They had probably foreseen that many among them would die, but they could face death more readily than shame. They fought for honor without regard for the overwhelming odds they faced. Defeat was a disappointing result but not completely unexpected; as decent farmfolk they lacked the taste for blood or tactical savvy to be victorious in a battle against fanatical foes who made killing their livelihood.

When the tide of battle began to turn against them, the tribesmen had requested American air support, but were denied. U.S. Forces couldn't afford to be seen publicly as favoring their former Sunni enemies, the Islamic sect of Saddam Hussein, by intervening in intertribal violence, or demean themselves by acquiescing to the requests of peasant folk. Block by block the insurgents pushed them back into the open desert, where they were scattered and slaughtered. No news cameras recorded their deaths. No reporters lauded their stubborn bravery or published their names and called them heroes. They died in the sand, abandoned to a hopeless fate, left to bleed and be eaten by scavengers. As cannon fodder they had performed as well as could be expected of them and in the end Husaybah remained in the clutches of the insurgents. One could not help but wonder what later became of the families the farmers left behind who with no patriarchs left to protect them were presumably left to the mercy of Al-Qaeda's vengeance.

Without a doubt there would be repercussions for the families, and not solely to make examples of them for their complicity with the Americans. The insurgents likely felt a need to compensate for their frustration in knowing that their relationship with the townspeople had forever been changed. They had won a single battle, but the fact they fought it at all was significant because it meant they could no longer rely on the favor of the people or even exploit their fear.

During lunch the next day, a television news program aired on the chow hall's big projection television with a story about Husaybah. There was no mention of the recent battle. It was a story about the Marines and their dogs.

I nudged Josh with my elbow.

"Look who it is!"

On the screen the puppies wagged their tails happily and trotted alongside their masters. I smiled to see that, at last, the media had chosen to show some good news about Iraq. It was hard to hear above the din of conversation. The reporter was talking to a young Marine whose sunburned face glowed with love for his pet.

But the Marines in the chow hall didn't share his joy. In fact, they seemed rather unimpressed. One of the men across the table looked over his shoulder, and with a mouth half-full of food asked, "You know what happened to those dogs, right?" He jabbed his fork toward the screen.

An odd question.

I shook my head questioningly. "What do you mean? We were just there."

The man replied matter-of-factly, turning back to his tray. "They made them throw all the dogs over the wall or shoot them. Said they were disease vectors."

I stirred my potatoes, no longer smiling.

So the rules had reached Camp Gannon after all.

I could tell the Marine wasn't pleased either, but he spoke with the level, unemotional tone of a man used to accepting the worst parts of life without complaint. It was not his place to question the decision to kill the dogs. Whoever had made it, it was simply another order to be obeyed. No point in being upset about something that couldn't be changed.

And why should he care?

It was on the home stretch of the tour for 3rd Battalion, 2nd Marines. Soon they would be back home with their loved ones where they could pretend the nightmare of Iraq had never happened, if it weren't for the stark absences of the dead Marines from their ranks. More and more troops from the replacement unit, 3rd Battalion, 6th Marines, arrived daily. Now that the reality of actually going home was finally imminent, it seemed frivolous to lament dead dogs while we still struggled with memories of men who weren't ever going home. No more big missions would be scheduled until after the transition. There was no reason to make waves, no reason to do anything to jeopardize one's chances of setting foot once more on American soil.

As for our TPT, the three of us had still not been informed by our headquarters of a firm redeployment date. Fresh faces arrived in Al Qa'im and old ones left, but we didn't know whether we were supposed to remain in Iraq for another month, or six. Living in limbo, not knowing, was almost worse than if we had known for certain we were supposed to stay for another year. Then, at least, we would have had a light at the end of the tunnel to look forward to. As it was, we didn't even know in which direction to look.

There was a vague sense of frustration and envy in watching the Marines we'd worked with for so long pack their things and leave. I felt left behind, both in space and time. It was like being asked to start the whole deployment over from the first day. Just as 3/2 had done when they first arrived, 3/6 would need to become familiar with the routes and towns we already knew so well, and through the crucible of combat grow gradually more jaded.

Suddenly, without warning, the low buzz of mealtime conversation was drowned out by a mighty, echoing *BOOOOM!*

The walls of the chow hall flexed and shivered, buffeted by the pressure wave of a massive explosion. To my ear it sounded like a Katyusha rocket had landed in the dirt lot just outside the chow hall. For a moment there was dead silence, as everyone's eyes grew wide and we stared at each other in disbelief. We were all instantly struck by the realization we were trapped in a tightly packed, confined space.

A perfect target for the enemy's rockets.

In the next second another, even louder explosion threw the chow hall into total chaos. The men tipped over their chairs and scattered in every direction. They threw themselves under tables and ran outside toward the safety of concrete bunkers, or into the kitchen to take cover behind the stoves and refrigerators. Abandoned trays and food coated the floor and tables in a slippery mess of squashed peas and spilled drinks.

We had to get outside.

The chow hall was only built of thin, corrugated metal. We couldn't risk being trapped inside if the roof collapsed. My mind considered a thousand different versions of the worst sort of frantic, panicked thoughts.

There is still a chance I won't make it home.

Uninvited visions of the dead pried their way into my brain.

But once outside, the Marines only milled around. Instead of diving for shelter, they stared into the sky at a pair of low-flying F-18 jets that had just broken the sound barrier as they streaked away. An army Special Forces soldier who had been walking to chow witnessed the confused scene unfold. He couldn't contain his cackling laughter.

I glared at the laughing man accusingly. He hadn't known the terror and confusion that still made my heart thrum in my chest, but I couldn't bear him any resentment. One had to find some humor in the whole mess that was our lives to maintain sanity, especially since we had no idea how much longer we would have to cope with living as we did.

I could at least feel some small measure of reassurance knowing that every day that passed was one day closer to the end, whether that end was death or reunion. I still wasn't ready to place my bet on either outcome, even if the latest attack had only been a cruel practical joke. I put my hand on my rapidly beating heart and breathed a deep sigh of relief.

It would be best to come back later for dinner, after the mess had been cleaned up.

My appetite had vanished anyway.

Proof of the passage of time hit home especially profoundly one day in September, when looking down from the turret as we prepared to leave the base for a routine meet-and-greet in one of the local villages, the new faces I counted outnumbered the old. More and more often 3rd Battalion, 6th Marines, integrated themselves into the missions as the men of 3rd Battalion, 2nd Marines, continued to filter back to the States. The changeover happened by degrees so small as to be hardly noticeable. By design it was meant to be imperceptible so that anyone observing movement to and from the base would not perceive an opportunity to exploit the seam between the new arrivals and outgoing Marines.

The slow transition also served another purpose. While the veterans still walked the same streets with newly in-country counterparts, the veterans had time to pass on as much knowledge and experience as possible and ensure solid continuity. The Marines called it the "left-seat, right-seat" phase of their relief in place process, a reference to the position of the troop

commander's seat on the right side of our Humvees as opposed to the driver's seat on the left. It signified the new battalion's graduation from taking
instructions to taking command.

The fresh replacements formally accepted responsibility for the whole
of 3/2's former area of operations in the following weeks, marked by a
transfer of authority ceremony behind the headquarters in which, with due
military pageantry, the new battalion colors were unfurled and the old ones
rolled and cased. The ceremony marked the point after which the newly
arrived Marines would choose their own path and, with reins firmly in
hand, prove their efficacy of their training.

As one of their final efforts in-country, the old battalion and a detachment of navy seabees had begun construction on several miniature forts
close to Karabilah and Ubaydi. It was intended that the so-called "battle
positions" would serve as staging areas from which the Marines could
maintain a permanent presence within the surrounding population centers
instead of abandoning towns after a few days of fighting, only to see them
quickly reclaimed by the insurgents, as had been our practice. The first
major operation planned by 3/6, nicknamed "Steel Curtain," intended
to resweep the insurgency from Husaybah, Karabilah, and Ubaydi, and
through occupation of the new forts deny militants the opportunity to
regain a foothold.

The decision to maintain an enduring presence in the towns signified
a hard-learned and fundamental change in the Marines' strategy due in
part to the changing attitudes of the Iraqi people. What happened in
Husaybah had only been one battle, but the fact that the tribesmen were
willing to die fighting Al-Qaeda indicated that Anbar's citizens were close
to the breaking point of their patience. Increasingly they proved their
willingness to repudiate the teachings of an organization led by foreign,
bloodthirsty, religious fanatics who sought to impose a twisted value system
on what had recently been a secular nation, whose primary goal was to kill
those who did not believe as they did. Terrorism and its cruelly indis-
criminate tactics were at last becoming more intolerable than the American
occupation, which at least promised to rebuild as much as it destroyed.

The common people were growing tired of living in fear. Calls to the
tips lines increased daily, as did the frequency of rocket and mortar strikes
on our bases. The spike in attacks, however, seemed more like an enemy's

desperate admission that their influence was fading than a display of strength.

I wanted to believe the changes meant hope still lived and I struggled to find in them some sense of purpose as motivation to continue caring.

The weeks dragged on.

In the last week of August 2005, Hurricane Katrina struck the Gulf Coast of the United States killing almost two thousand people and causing billions of dollars in damage. Among the army units sent to Louisiana to assist in the recovery efforts was the company that had previously been slated to replace ours in Iraq.

There was no longer any indication how long it would be before anyone came to relieve us. No one debated the importance of helping fellow Americans in need. But, after looking forward so long to going home, while watching the Marines of 3/2 leave us behind, and then being told that redeployment was further away than we'd thought struck a bitter blow to our team's morale. As more information about the devastating extent of the hurricane damage became clear, it was rumored that Charlie Company's rotation might be extended several months, possibly even until January.

"Great. I was supposed to get out of the army in January. I guess that means I'll be stop-lossed," I grumbled to Josh upon hearing the news.

I resigned myself to fate and waiting. I hated myself for thinking it, but with every extension our mission felt less like a job that might someday end and more like a deferred death sentence. Missions with 3/6 were like déjà vu from the first days of our deployment. I noticed as well that my sense of self-preservation was draining away into dangerous apathy; I had finally, completely accepted the fact that an infinite deployment made my death inevitable. I was at peace with the fact I had lived a full-enough life and was no more deserving of the opportunity to make plans for my future than the men who'd been killed before me. I remained vigilant only to protect the lives of my friends.

To my surprise, however, instead of enduring an eternity of combat in Iraq I was one of a handful of soldiers nearing the end of their enlistments who were slated to return to the United States in advance of the rest of the company's still-to-be-determined redeployment. I considered reenlistment briefly out of feelings of guilt for leaving my team behind, but deep down I knew that if presented the opportunity, I would selfishly choose escape. I would go home, leave the army having fulfilled my four-year obligation, and finish college with the GI Bill as I'd always planned.

I've done enough, haven't I? What more can the army expect of me? I shouldn't feel guilty about not wanting to be party to more killing. I don't understand why I do. Will my teammates think I have abandoned them? Why do I feel guilty that I survived, when so many other men died? I should be thankful that for me, it's over. I should be proud that I've done all that was asked of me.

But I didn't feel the way I wanted to. I didn't feel the feelings my reasoning told me I should feel. I felt small, and selfish, and alone, as if in leaving the danger my friends still faced, I betrayed them.

Josh walked with me to the helicopter the day I left Al Qa'im. We pretended it was a day like any other, and he helped me carry my bags through the rotor wash and up the ramp. Only after I stood facing him inside the kerosene-scented bay, knowing I might never see him again, was I overcome by a tsunami of emotion. I extended my hand to say good-bye, but my remorseful heart forced me to draw him into a tight embrace instead.

"You are my brother," I shouted over the rotors, tearfully.

He simply nodded. "I'll see you back home, Russ. Be safe."

"Wait!" I reached inside the Velcro flap of my body armor and unpinned a small gold crucifix, hidden there many months before. It was simple but personally immensely meaningful, a gift from my mother meant to protect me. A tiny mustard seed was encased in a clear plastic bubble in the center of the cross. I held it in my palm, offering the talisman to my friend. The feeling of intense loneliness rose achingly in my chest, as if I were abandoning the only family I'd ever known.

How could I forgive myself if something happened to him, and I did not share his suffering?

"My mom gave me this crucifix. It protected me. I think it should stay here with you."

According to a parable attributed to Jesus, as related in the New Testament's book of Matthew, with faith as small as a mustard seed you could move a mountain.

What if the cross had protected me? Could I, even though the rational side of my mind doubted the existence of God, deny the possibility of its protection to my friends?

Though only a tiny speck the seed signified my hope that Josh and Stephenson might enjoy divine protection, the wish we all might one day be reunited and find peace within ourselves, and the anticipation that someday men like us might never again have to face each other in war.

At the same time I felt immense relief that my experience in Iraq was all but over, and I had survived. The transference of the crucifix felt symbolic and final. Death had passed his scythe over me, but I still stood, unharmed. I was headed home to forget about the past months' carnage, if I could, and wouldn't have to carry a weapon or wonder if the last day of my life might arrive sooner than I hoped. I could sleep without fear of a mortar coming through the roof, or of being paralyzed by a roadside bomb, or having my face burned away. I was one of the fortunate ones. I bore no *physical* scars to remind me of the past eight months, which at times had truly been a waking nightmare. Yet, I knew I would never be the same man I once had been.

As the chopper lifted trembling into the air, the earth fell away into a haze and with it, a great weight seemed to drop from my shoulders. I was free. I was alive. I entered into a second chapter of my life, a divine gift miraculously spared from all the worst of war and yet somehow I didn't feel worthy, having left so many shattered, more deserving lives behind. I wanted to forget everything I'd seen, to close my eyes and absolve myself of the nagging guilt and memories of blood. The chopper flew on. Attached to the weight, an invisible chain unraveled from the very depths of my soul, anchoring me forever to Al Qa'im.

In Memoriam

Derived from my own memories and contemporaneous notes, this book is closely based on actual events that occurred during Operation Iraqi Freedom in Al Anbar Province, Iraq, between March and October 2005. As a result of these actions at least fifty-three Marines, two navy corpsmen, and hundreds of Iraqis were killed. Their final hours bore testament to the basest savageries of which humanity is capable; yet in spite of the evil which surrounded them they witnessed, too, man's potential for selflessness. During their lives they never knew a world without war, but moved by their deaths, I pray with stubborn optimism that someday a future generation might never know a world without peace.